Scarecrow Film Score Guides
Series Editor: Kate Daubney

Miklós Rózsa's
Ben-Hur

A Film Score Guide

Roger Hickman

Scarecrow Film Score Guides, No. 10

The Scarecrow Press, Inc.
Lanham, Maryland • Toronto • Plymouth, UK
2011

SCARECROW PRESS, INC.

Published in the United States of America
by Scarecrow Press, Inc.
A wholly owned subsidary of
The Rowman & Littlefield Publishing Group, Inc.
4501 Forbes Boulevard, Suite 200, Lanham, Maryland 20706
www.scarecrowpress.com

Estover Road
Plymouth PL6 7PY
United Kingdom

British Library Cataloguing in Publication Information Available

Library of Congress Cataloging-in-Publication Data
Hickman, Roger.
 Miklós Rózsa's Ben-Hur : a film score guide / Roger Hickman.
  p. cm. — (Scarecrow film score guides ; no. 10)
 Includes bibliographical references and index.
 ISBN 978-0-8108-8100-6 (pbk. : alk. paper)
 1. Rózsa, Miklós, 1907–1995. Ben-Hur. I. Title.
 ML410.R883H53 2011
 781.5'42–dc22   2010051726

To Maureen

*For being the Esther in my life
and leading me to a rediscovery of* Ben-Hur

CONTENTS

ILLUSTRATIONS AND TABLES

Examples

Tables

EDITOR'S FOREWORD

As the Scarecrow Film Score Guides enter their second decade since the publication of the series' first volume (for Greenwood) in 2000 on Max Steiner's score for *Now, Voyager*, the contrast between the three volumes to be published in 2011 offers us a fascinating opportunity to reflect on the accomplishments of the series thus far. Between the classic black-and-white intensity of *Rebecca*, the epic scope of *Ben-Hur*, and the modern unities of the *Three Colours* trilogy, one can triangulate the enormous possibilities for film as a complex storytelling machine, and within that the extraordinary richness that music adds and enables within that narrative intention. Not only do these three volumes take us on a mini-journey through the evolution of scoring techniques, but they also remind us of many of the constants we carry with us as listeners of film scores that are both fulfilled and challenged with every new film we experience. The series was established to promote score-focused scholarship, but that simple aim has long since been outstripped by the achievements of the series' authors in divulging great variety in what the analysis of these constants might consist of. There have been revisions of our understanding of some of the figureheads of film score composition and revelations of the logistics of their compositional practice. The impact of technology on scoring has been exposed from both its early manifestations as instrumentation to its impact on process. Some canonic score sounds that have permanently permeated the public consciousness have been deconstructed, and bewitching and byzantine aural textures have been explored in critical and theoretical ways that push the boundaries of music out into the wider soundscape of film.

The series' authors have unpicked and rewoven some of the fabric of the earlier 'schools' of film musicology, and many have become leading scholars in the discipline as a consequence of contributing volumes to this series. So much has been illuminated in so many different ways, and yet what binds these volumes together is an essential engagement in our experience of music in film and a fascination for the means by which we are drawn in. That original principle behind the establishment of the series has remained largely unchanged, even if the disciplinary environment in which the work is undertaken has evolved as a consequence of the work itself.

One of the great challenges in any analysis of creative work is to return to well-known and well-loved works with fresh eyes in order to find new perspectives and explore how changing analytical frameworks might open up new interpretations. *Ben-Hur* is a story which itself has had many revisitings in theatrical and cinematic form, and it is difficult, given the scale of the epic film analyzed in this book, not to think that somehow this particular *Ben-Hur* might be the definitive interpretation of Lew Wallace's original novel. Certainly for Miklós Rózsa, now considered the master of composing for the biblical epic, there must have been a gathering sense that the larger the scale of the film, the greater the burden on the score to enhance still further that seemingly unbounded vision of the wide screen. Indeed, *Ben-Hur* is among that generation of films which revisited the significance of the great historical tales by exploding the magnitude with which their detail could be represented, and that is reflected with utterly delicate synergy in Rózsa's construction of the score's organic components. Dr. Hickman guides us carefully through the layers of meaning and interpretation of first the story and then the music, so that we can appreciate the craftsmanship of a score that both upholds the tradition of thematic precision of Rózsa's predecessors such as Max Steiner, but also does great narrative justice to the elements of the story. This is a score of epic proportions too, and so whatever the level of musical knowledge of the reader, this book upholds the legacy of all its predecessors in the last decade by providing much that will illuminate the enjoyment of this favorite and distinctive film.

Dr. Kate Daubney
Series Editor

ACKNOWLEDGMENTS

The publication of this study on Miklós Rózsa and his music for *Ben-Hur* marks the end of a lengthy and remarkably enjoyable journey. The research and writing process involved support from a number of individuals and institutions. I would like to begin by thanking the staff at Scarecrow Press. Kate Daubney has been a thoughtful and thorough series editor. Your patience, perceptive observations, and positive attitude are warmly appreciated. Renée Camus was a great asset in the selection of this subject, and Stephen Ryan, Christen Karniski, and Sally Craley have effectively guided the completion of the project.

The research for this study was made possible through a sabbatical leave granted by California State University, Long Beach. In particular, I would like to thank Don Para, former Dean of the College of Arts and now Provost for the University, for your constant support through my twenty plus years in the music department. I would also like to acknowledge the encouragement from the music chairman John Carnahan and the practical expertise and assistance from my musicological colleague Kris Forney.

The work in various libraries has been a most pleasurable experience. The University of Syracuse houses the largest collection of Rózsa manuscripts, and its staff was remarkably responsive and patient with my many needs. I found similar support at the Library of Congress and at the music and film libraries for the Academy of Motion Picture Arts and Sciences, the University of Southern California, and the University of California, Los Angeles.

A final special thanks is due to William Rosar. You are a living treasure with your knowledge of film music, your understanding of the field, and your passion for the subject. I have learned much from your honest criticisms, discussions via email and over coffee, and precise editing. And, needless-to-say, you were more than generous in lending me your personal copy of the *Ben-Hur* score for these several years.

INTRODUCTION

Hollywood's "Golden Age" of filmmaking boasted an impressive roster of composers that included Max Steiner, Alfred Newman, Herbert Stothart, Erich Korngold, Franz Waxman, and Dimitri Tiomkin. In 1941, two new figures entered the Hollywood scene; Bernard Herrmann created an immediate sensation with the music for *Citizen Kane* and *All That Money Can Buy*, and the Hungarian-born Miklós Rózsa wrote his first American film scores, receiving Oscar nominations for *Lydia* and *Sundown*. Herrmann and Rózsa would remain active in the industry for over three decades. Both would retain some autonomy with the studios, and both were committed to writing music for concert hall performances.

Their careers would coincide with the decline of the Hollywood studio system and with fundamental changes in attitudes towards film music. Through the shifting musical tastes of filmmakers and audiences, Herrmann and Rózsa were able to sustain high-quality film scores. Herrmann became a leading figure in developing a more contemporary sound in American movies. Rózsa also contributed to the expanding role of dissonance and color during the 1940s in films such as *Double Indemnity*, *Spellbound*, and *A Double Life*. But he did not stray too far from established Hollywood clichés and soon forged a successful blend of modern and romantic qualities. During this latter "neo-Romantic" phase, Rózsa composed the music for *Ben-Hur*, his defining masterpiece and one of the finest scores in the history of Hollywood filmmaking.

This book focuses on the confluence of traditions, trends, and innovations that shaped the score of *Ben-Hur*. The approach to this material is taken from a musicological perspective, but the term musicology, of course, encompasses such a wide variety of attitudes that some refinement is required. During my graduate days at U.C. Berkeley, there was a strong movement to refer to the field as "music history" rather than musicology. I supported such a revision, since the new label touched on my two primary interests—history and music. These two areas have since governed my research and serve as the guiding principles of this study.

Ben-Hur occupies several significant historical positions. The film stands as the last major manifestation of the most commercially successful story of the twentieth century. The original novel by Lew Wallace set sales records in America that would only be surpassed by *Gone With the Wind*. The stage play based on the novel was an international sensation, and the silent film adaptation established MGM as Hollywood's grandest studio. The popularity and spectacle of the stage play influenced another twentieth-century artistic cycle—epic films based on stories set in antiquity. The traditions of this genre, established in the silent film era and sustained through the early 1930s, were revitalized in 1949. *Ben-Hur* appears at the crest of a wave of biblical epics that were among Hollywood's most successful films of the decade.

In many respects, Rózsa's music for *Ben-Hur* also represents the end of the Golden Age of Hollywood film music. Although there were a number of excellent full symphonic scores in the 1960s, including Rózsa's own *El Cid*, *Ben-Hur* stands as the last universally acknowledged score created in the classical Hollywood tradition prior to *Star Wars* (1977). In turn, it would become one of the most influential scores on the *Star Wars* generation. The critical success of this unabashedly conservative film score for its time is due in part to Rózsa's ability to write in a contemporary musical idiom while maintaining a direct, emotional appeal to general audiences. Ultimately, it is this musical synthesis that defines Rózsa's greatness as a film composer.

The discussion of music—what are the outstanding features of the score, what are the qualities of contemporary and romantic music, why does the music succeed within the context of the film—is a formidable challenge. These matters cannot be addressed without delving into detail, and this makes for tedious reading, even for those with extensive musical backgrounds. Two issues complicate this task even further. The first and most serious is the unavailability of a library score of this music that could be consulted while reading. One can easily imagine the difficulty in reading Joseph Kerman's book on the Beethoven string quartets without being able to view the scores. This remains the foremost obstacle facing historians in the field of film music today. Knowing that most readers will have access only to the film itself, I have tried to include as many musical excerpts as possible to aid the process. Ultimately, we all look forward to a time when scores like *Ben-Hur* are readily available in university libraries.

The second issue is the need in this score to analyze neo-tonal music. Several years are devoted to teaching music students the process and terminology of functional tonal music, in which central key areas are defined through the cadential progression of a dominant-seventh chord resolving to a tonic. Neo-tonality, the compositional technique of defining a tonal center without a dominant-seventh, is the subject of less scrutiny and fewer clearly defined terms. I have tried to move beyond the generalities that often accompany discussions of contemporary idioms. Although the concepts may seem complicated, they are relatively simple ideas that are obscured mostly through unfamiliarity. I have also attempted to strike a balance between everything that could be said about a subject and what can be easily understood. For the most part, general concepts are followed by supporting details in order to allow the reader to delve into multiple levels of understanding as desired. For those that are unacquainted with the terminology of modern music, explanatory footnotes are added in the earlier chapters with the intention that they could be consulted while reading later chapters.

The consideration of *Ben-Hur*'s historical positions and discussions of music are interrelated subjects that appear in all five chapters. The first two provide an overview of Rózsa's music into the 1960s. Chapter 1 looks at Rózsa's musical influences and the development of his distinctive style, primarily focusing on his concert music. Chapter 2 deals specifically with how Rózsa applied these compositional techniques to film scoring. Both chapters are organized around the three major phases of Rózsa's career: the establishment of a Hungarian nationalist style, the challenge of modernity in the mid-1940s, and the emergence of a mature neo-Romantic style in the 1950s.

The next three chapters address *Ben-Hur* more directly. Chapter 3 explores the *Ben-Hur* phenomenon and traces the development of the story and its musical traditions from the original novel into the twenty-first century. Chapter 4 examines the conventions of epic films set in

antiquity beginning with the silent film era. Chapter 5 ties these influences together with a detailed analysis of the score. The analysis in this
chapter follows the chronology of the plot, which necessitates some
description. Still, this is the most accessible approach for a score of this
size, and it engenders a greater appreciation of Rózsa's masterful han-
dling of divergent materials and his strong sense of unity.

    In a casual conversation with a good friend, the question arose
about how one could write an entire book just on the music for *Ben-
Hur*. My immediate response was to wonder how one could limit the
subject to just one volume. There are so many topics and perspectives
that one could apply to this subject. My task was eased by the appearance of several earlier studies that have explored both the composer and
the music to *Ben-Hur* in detail. Christopher Palmer employs insights
gained from his personal knowledge of the composer and his outstanding musical background to a biography and several overviews of
Rózsa's works. Ralph Erkelenz has provided an exhaustive examination of the *Ben-Hur* manuscript score in five installments appearing in
Pro Musica Sana, published by the Miklós Rózsa Society. His detail
and accuracy have made it possible for this study to move into different
realms. *Pro Musica Sana*, which is edited by John Fitzpatrick and has
strong contributions from Frank DeWald, Mark Koldys, and Derek
Elley, is a source of considerable information and insights into Rózsa's
music and the Hollywood scene. Another major figure in Rózsa scholarship is Steven Wescott, who created a landmark study with his 1990
dissertation from the University of Minnesota. In addition, a chapter by
Wescott in *Film Music* focuses specifically on Rózsa's use of leitmotifs
in *Ben-Hur*. His observations are astute, and the work is recommended
for additional thoughts and, at times, different perspectives on this
score.

    The history and music of *Ben-Hur* are fascinating subjects. In spite
of the publication of this "entire book" and the quality of previous studies, the topics surrounding Rózsa and *Ben-Hur* are hardly exhausted. I
look forward to the appearance of further work in the area giving fresh
insights and new interpretations. The score for *Ben-Hur* is brilliantly
conceived, and its story reveals much about movies and musical life in
twentieth-century America.

1

MIKLÓS RÓZSA'S
MUSICAL BACKGROUND

Miklós Rózsa is one of the leading figures of the second generation of Hollywood film composers. Born in Budapest in 1907, Rózsa published his Opus 1 in 1927, just as the silent era was coming to a close. His first film scores were created in England in 1937, and he moved to Hollywood three years later, where he eventually became the most prestigious composer on the staff at MGM. In 1957, this studio chose William Wyler to direct a new production of *Ben-Hur*, its most ambitious project of the decade. At this time, Rózsa was fifty years old, a published composer for thirty years, and a veteran of film music for twenty. He began work on the *Ben-Hur* score during the following year, and the success of the film and its music would mark a financial high point for the studio during its declining years and the pinnacle of Rózsa's career as a composer.

On the lengthy journey to this summit, Rózsa absorbed numerous influences, many of which are detailed in his engaging autobiography entitled *Double Life*.[1] Borrowed from the film *A Double Life*, the title refers to his split between two professional worlds—film composer and concert composer. This perceived bifurcation provided a framework for his career, but the two lives were closely intertwined. Both grew musically from his Hungarian roots, both were challenged by a modernity crisis, and both found an ultimate synthesis in a neo-Romantic style that retained characteristics of contemporary music and communicated with general audiences. During the latter phase Rózsa produced some of his most universally acclaimed compositions, including the score for *Ben-Hur*.

Hungarian Nationalism

Hungary

Rózsa was born at a time when Hungary was in political, social, and musical disarray. Tied to the Hapsburgs, Hungary shared in Austria's political setbacks. Both regions were stunned by the assassinations of Queen Elisabeth in 1898 and Archduke Franz Ferdinand, the heir to the throne, in 1914. Austria-Hungary responded to the latter event by declaring war on Serbia, marking the beginning of World War I. At the end of this disastrous conflict, Hungary was carved up; over two-thirds of its territory was divided between Austria, Czechoslovakia, Romania, and the Kingdom of Serbs, Croats, and Slovenes. These humiliating new borders were finalized in 1920, while Rózsa was just entering his teens.

Prior to this partitioning, the Kingdom of Hungary had ruled over numerous diverse ethnic cultures, and there was a strong political movement to compel people of other ethnic origins to adopt the Hungarian language and culture. The quest for a national identity affected Hungarian music greatly. In the early years of the twentieth century, however, this identity would be elusive. Concert music stemming from the traditions of Franz Liszt remained largely Germanic and would soon be challenged by modernism. Concurrently, authentic peasant music was dissipating, as the demands of mass culture for "gypsy" music threatened to obscure genuine folk traditions. The issue of *Magyarsag* (Hungarianness) in music was the subject of lengthy debates with no clear resolution.

The generation of Hungarian composers preceding Rózsa dealt with these issues in vastly different ways. Two leading figures, Leo Weiner (1885-1960) and Ernö Dohnányi (1877-1960), wrote primarily in Germanic forms. Both studied and eventually taught at the Budapest Academy of Music. Weiner, who excelled at chamber music, retained strong ties to late romanticism. Dohnányi was acknowledged internationally as one of the finest pianists of his generation, and he enjoyed a varied career as concert artist, conductor, composer, and teacher. His works show an eclectic mixture of romantic, modern, and occasional folk qualities, as evident in his humorous *Variations on a Nursery Song* for Piano and Orchestra, Opus 25. But as Rózsa pointed out, this work is "far removed from any Hungarian feeling."[2]

While Weiner and Dohnányi worked in the prevailing international style, folk music served as a source for the works of the two most prominent Hungarian composers of the twentieth century, Zoltán Kodály (1882-1967) and Béla Bartók (1881-1945). Rejecting the influence of traditional Western art music and the growing popularization of gypsy music, both collected and recorded songs from remote villages. In these melodies, Kodály recognized the critical role played by pentatonic scales,[3] which he describes as "the basis of the music of so many ancient people, perhaps of all peoples."[4] Using a theoretical model based on G, he observed that the ranges of Hungarian folk melodies generally vary from a fifth (G, B-flat, C, D) to an eleventh (F, G, B-flat, C, D, F, G, B-flat). When the range extends below the home pitch, the pentatonic scale has a modal sound derived from the cadential motion of F to G, a unifying gesture in the score for *Ben-Hur*.

The third movement of the *Háry János* Suite (1926-1927) typifies Kodály's adaptation of folk characteristics into his concert music. It opens with an authentic folk melody. The two phrases of the tune encompass the range of a tenth and are divided into two-measure units with no metric irregularities. The pitches are drawn from a pentatonic scale. The only note in the first phrase (Example 1.1) that lies outside of the scale is the B-natural in measure three, which Kodály would consider to be a passing tone.

Example 1.1. Kodály, *Háry János* Suite, III.

Each two-measure unit (marked with brackets) has a range of a perfect fourth or fifth with a prominent intervening major second (these pitches are noted with an "x"). This figure, which will be referred to in this study as the "cell" motive, can also be found in the works of Bartók, such as *Bluebeard's Castle* and the *Concerto for Orchestra*.

Other folklike qualities in this melody include the Scottish snaps[5] and the dark, plaintive timbre of the viola soloist. These elements, along with the reliance on the pentatonic scale and the cell motive, will be fundamental to the emerging nationalist style of Rózsa. The remainder of Kodály's movement has additional parallels to Rózsa's later works, including triadic-oriented harmony, colorful orchestrations, skilled variation techniques, and strong emotional appeal.

Bartók undertook his first folk-song collecting expedition in the year of Rózsa's birth. Like Kodály, Bartók incorporated aspects of peasant music into his compositions, but he included a wider variety of folk traditions. Indeed, he was attacked in 1920 for promoting Romanian culture, and hence being a traitor to Hungary. Bartók developed a stronger link to modernist tendencies, resulting in a high degree of dissonance, freely shifting meters, and declamatory melodies. When Rózsa began searching for a more modern voice, the music of Bartók would serve as a model. But for his early concert and film music, Rózsa would have a stronger affinity with Kodály.

Rózsa's Early Works

Rózsa's family background gave him a dual legacy. His father came from the country and became a successful land-owning industrialist. As a politically minded liberal, he gave much thought to the social issues of the time. Before Miklós was born, he wrote a book entitled *To Whom Does the Hungarian Soil Belong?* Miklós' mother studied piano at the Budapest Academy and was just two classes behind Bartók. Although she did not pursue a career in music after marriage, she provided a strong musical presence at home. Here the young Miklós would absorb Hungarian folk songs sung by his father and the piano music of Franz Liszt performed by his mother.

This early double life was also reflected in the family's two homes. During much of the year, Miklós lived comfortably in Budapest. He began to study the violin at the age of five and started composing by seven. But for the summer months, he stayed in the family estate at the foot of the Mátra Mountains, the home of an indigenous Magyar people known as the Palóc. "It was the music of the Palóc that I heard during those summers I spent on the estate and that intrigued me from my earliest childhood, although of course it wasn't until later that I realized what a vital shaping force it was proving on my own musical personality."[6]

Foregoing the continuation of his education in Budapest and the possibility of working with Kodály,[7] Rózsa went to the Leipzig Conservatory of Music in 1926, where he studied with Hermann Grabner. A former student of Max Reger, Grabner possessed two attributes of a good teacher: he did not favor a particular method of composing, and hence encouraged Rózsa to develop his own style, and he actively promoted Rózsa's early career. Through a mutual friend, he helped Rózsa publish his String Trio, Opus 1 (1927) and Piano Quintet, Opus 2 (1928) with Breitkopf und Härtel.

There are some hints of Hungarian nationalism in these two works: Scottish snaps, strong accents on second beats, and several pentatonic themes. But for the most part, they are Germanic and exhibit neo-classic qualities: four-movement structures, classical forms, clear tonal centers, triadic-based harmonies, and substantial contrapuntal activity. Nancy McKenney notes that these are Rózsa's only chamber works to employ key signatures and suggests that their style is derived from Richard Strauss and Max Reger.[8] One should also consider the influence of Paul Hindemith. According to Rózsa, he was the most highly regarded composer in Leipzig at this time:

> The reigning master of contemporary music was Paul Hindemith, a brilliant viola player who wrote two concertos for the instrument, which he himself performed all over the country. His operas, chamber music, and orchestral works were played everywhere, and his influence on young composers was enormous. They all imitated his style but none achieved his brilliance.[9]

Rózsa would share a number of convictions with Hindemith; both felt a strong sense of the composer's duty to communicate with the general public, and both were critical of Schoenberg and the New Viennese School. In succeeding years, parallels between the music of Rózsa and Hindemith continued, such as their use of quartal chords, parallel harmony, and the ultimate supremacy of triads.

In 1929, Breitkopf und Härtel published three additional works by Rózsa: Rhapsody for Cello and Orchestra, Opus 3; *Variations on a Hungarian Peasant Song*, Opus 4; and *North Hungarian Peasant Songs and Dances*, Opus 5. A sharp break in style occurs with Rózsa's inclusion of folk elements in the latter two. In a reference to his Rhapsody, Rózsa notes: "Stylistically, it is a transitional piece, still much influenced by Germanic prototypes. But the more contemporary German music I heard, the more I became aware that it wasn't for me. I wanted to go back to my origins, to Hungarian folk song, and this is exactly what I did in my next two works."[10] The Hungarian folk qualities in these works, perhaps due to their setting for a solo violin with accompaniment, also reflect some influence of Gypsy music.

During the early 1930s, Rózsa composed two significant orchestral works: *Serenade*, Opus 10 (1932, revised in 1946 as *Hungarian Serenade*, Opus 25) and *Theme, Variations and Finale*, Opus 13 (1933), which earned him his first international recognition. *Theme, Variations and Finale* received performances throughout Europe and the United

States under the batons of several podium titans. Bruno Walter scheduled a performance of *Theme, Variations and Finale* for a nationally broadcast performance by the New York Philharmonic at Carnegie Hall on November 14, 1943. In the celebrated twist of fate, Walter became ill at the last moment, and young Leonard Bernstein stepped in to conduct this historic concert that launched his conducting career and gave Rózsa his widest exposure as a concert composer.

The opening melody for *Theme, Variations and Finale* is not an authentic folk tune, but it has a character similar to the Kodály theme from the *Háry János* Suite (compare Examples 1.1 and 1.2). An unaccompanied oboe initially presents Rózsa's theme (a solo oboe plays the melody in the first variation of Kodály's movement), and the tempo designations for both include the term "rubato." The range of Rózsa's melody is a ninth and, like Kodály's, can be divided into several motivic units that are subject to later imitation and variation.

Example 1.2. *Theme, Variations and Finale*, **Opening.**

The first measure contains a "cell" motive with the range of a fourth and an intervening major second. The second measure has a similar contour and also lies within the range of a perfect fourth. The pitches of these two measures, other than the expressive F, form part of a pentatonic scale. The third measure condenses the material of the first two and leads to a cadence (measure four) that repeats the motive of measure two and introduces a B-flat. This pitch prepares for the change to a new pentatonic scale in the next four measures (B-flat, C, D, F, and G).

A half-note cadence occurs every two measures. The pitches of the half notes (C, G, F, and G) outline a cell motive with a perfect fifth and major second. Isolating the last three of these half notes produces the defining modal gesture that achieves prominence in *Ben-Hur* (the descent and rise of a major second, as at the beginning of Example 4.2c).

The remainder of the work shows the hand of an accomplished composer. The placement of several variations in slow tempos followed by a scherzo variation creates the effect of a four-movement classical work. Qualities that can be found in later film scores include the colorful treatment of each section of the orchestra, a strong emotional content, the enrichment of texture through counterpoint, the lack of a key signature, and a rich harmonic palette that includes harsh minor-second dissonances and parallel triads.

At a climactic point just prior to rehearsal number 31, Rózsa introduces four reiterated chords in syncopation. While the lower instruments play an open fifth, the middle register strings contain two overlapping fifths, A-E and D-A (Example 1.3), creating a three-pitched quartal chord (E, A, D).[11] Rózsa employs this type of chord frequently in his later works; other than octave duplications, Example 1.3 is identical to the first chord of *Ben-Hur* (see Example 4.2a).

Example 1.3. *Theme, Variations and Finale*, **Chord.**

Theme, Variations and Finale may owe a debt to Kodály, but Rózsa's last published orchestral work of the 1930s, *Three Hungarian Sketches* (1938), embraces more fully the style of Bartók. Rózsa employs shifting meters, energetic dance rhythms, pentatonic melodies, colorful orchestrations that suggest folk music, and adventurous harmonic treatment, including parallel chords and four-note quartal chords. This work appeared in print just as Rózsa began to learn the craft of film music. Some of these qualities were carried over into his new field, but it was the more conservative nationalist style of *Theme, Variations and Finale* that best served the needs of his early film scores.

Rózsa acknowledged the formative role of Hungarian nationalism on his film music: "However much I may modify my style in order to write effectively for films, the music of Hungary is stamped indelibly one way or other on virtually every bar I have ever put on paper."[12] The metric regularity, colorful orchestration, clear pitch centers, and the easily developed modal and pentatonic thematic materials of his early nationalist concert works were easily adapted into film scores. With these materials, Rózsa was able to generate a wide variety of musical styles ranging from exotic and antique settings to moods for dark, psychologically disturbed individuals. Rózsa's Hungarian nationalism is an approach that allowed Rózsa great flexibility in both style and level of modernity. Although discussing quartal harmonies in the film music of Leith Stevens, Bill Rosar touches upon the flexibility of the Hungarian nationalist style:

> Whether derived from Hungarian folk song, Debussy, Ravel, Hindemith, Berg, Schoenberg, or Stravinsky, the use of quartal harmony by Stevens and his colleagues exhibits a common underlying expressive character that connects its use and similar-sounding sonorities in the Biblical films with their use in film noir: Quartal sonorities possess a distinctive musical physiognomy that very well may readily evoke a sense of the ancient, the primeval or primordial, and the primitive.[13]

Rózsa learned much from the works of Bartók, Kodály, and Hindemith. But like so many Hollywood composers, the orchestration techniques and harmonic practices (neo-tonality, complex chord structures, parallel harmonic movement) of Debussy, Ravel, and Stravinsky also had a large impact on his work, as did, by extension, similar techniques in the works of diverse composers such as Rimsky-Korsakov, Vaughan Williams, Respighi, and Bloch. But for a specific model for film music, Rózsa would look initially to the music of Arthur Honegger.

The Double Life Begins

Paris

Rózsa moved to Paris in 1931, where he wrote both songs and fanfares for Pathé. Following a joint concert with Honegger in 1934, the French composer invited Rózsa to view *Les Misérables*, for which he had provided music. Rózsa was impressed and would later use this film as the inspiration for his own scoring. Swynnoe duly notes: "Honegger may not have been the most appropriate model for a composer who was preparing to score British films."[14] Her assessment is certainly accurate for someone preparing to compose for Hollywood as well. But these observations avoid the more intriguing issues of what Rózsa saw in Honegger's score and how this admiration was manifested in his own music.

Undoubtedly, Rózsa was attracted to the French film because it is based on a classic novel, the type of movie that invariably excited Rózsa during his career. Honegger's cues are modest in number, but they enhance the varied emotions of the story well. The orchestration is economical and effective, especially in the darker passages that feature bass clarinet solos. Although Rózsa is best remembered for his large colorful orchestrations, he composed many intimate cues that contain similar subtle coloring. The sound of the bass clarinet was a particular favorite for Rózsa in his film noir scores.

Perhaps the most striking aspect of Honegger's music is the use of reiterated pulses. For the death of Jean Valjean, Honegger generates a great sense of poignancy through the dissonances and a persistent heartbeat pulse. A grander effect is achieved at the end of Part II, where the march first heard during the titles returns with a powerful crescendo as Jean and Cosette watch guards whipping convicts traveling in wagons. A similar intensity of sound is heard during the dramatic sewer scene at the climax of the film. As will be noted in more detail in chapter 2, Rózsa would incorporate marches into almost all of his early films, and the march would continue to play a prominent role in scores as diverse as *Double Indemnity* and *El Cid*. It is not difficult to hear echoes of Honegger's convict march in *Ben-Hur* during Christ's procession to Calgary while being whipped by guards.

Honegger's marches, as well as other symphonic cues, were easily adapted into concert works, a financial bonus that was not lost on Rózsa. He writes in his autobiography that he advised Honegger to make a suite out of the score to *Les Misérables*. The French master probably did not need the suggestion, since he had already crafted a suite from his music for *Napoléon* (1927) and would soon produce another for *Les Misérables*. In the succeeding decades, Rózsa would seemingly have an eye on the concert hall while composing film scores, a lesson that he likely learned from Honegger.

The ease of transforming film music into concert works largely depends upon the composer's stylistic integrity. In the music for *Les Misérables*, Honegger did not sacrifice or compromise his own distinctive style. Within his moderately dissonant idiom, he was able to create the emotions necessary for a given film. The music for *Les Misérables* demonstrated that modern techniques of concert music could succeed in the creation of a film score, an issue that would greatly concern Rózsa and many of his Hollywood colleagues. Rózsa assuredly had Honegger in mind when he wrote: "Russian and pre-war French films showed already remarkable dramatic effects achieved by modern composers with modern music."[15]

London and Hollywood

There are several landmark years in Rózsa's double life. The first is 1937, the year of his thirtieth birthday. By this time, Rózsa, now a resident in London, had developed an individual Hungarian nationalist style and had achieved meaningful success with concert music. In 1937, the city of Budapest awarded Rózsa the Franz Joseph Prize. This honor coincides with the composition of his first film scores, written for the Hungarian émigré Alexander Korda at London Films, one of England's largest studios. Rózsa learned his new trade through practical experience. Within three years, he scored seven films in a variety of genres, including comedy, romance, thriller, and adventure. Among these films are "the two finest achievements of Korda's last years at Denham:"[16] *Knight Without Armour* (1937) and *The Four Feathers* (1939).

Rózsa's next major assignment was to provide music for the fantasy *The Thief of Bagdad* (1940). Work on the film was complicated by the onset of World War II, and Korda went to the United States to complete the project. The film was in its final stages, when Korda decided that two scenes had to be redone. Many in the crew were asked to come to California, including Rózsa. Once the project was completed, Rózsa found ample work in his new home. Since Korda had close ties with United Artists and Paramount, these two studios would account for most of Rózsa's scoring assignments during his early Hollywood years.

Rózsa's double life achieved another milestone in 1943. During this year, Rózsa had his greatest concert-hall triumph with the Bernstein nationally broadcast performance of *Theme, Variations and Finale*, and his reputation in Hollywood got a substantial boost when RCA Victor issued an album of his music for *Jungle Book*, the first such recording of an American film score. From this point forward, it would be difficult to sustain both lives simultaneously. Actively working on film scores, he had little time left for writing concert music. Hence, Rózsa's most productive periods as a concert composer are prior to his double life (compositions through *Three Hungarian Sketches*), during lulls in his Hollywood commissions, and after his MGM contract expired in 1962. Beginning in the mid-1940s, the challenge of modernity would impact both of these lives substantially.

The Modernity Crises

Hollywood and Modern Music

Hollywood studios enjoyed the idea of having prestigious contemporary composers working for them, but they did not care much for modern music in their films. Partially as a result of this contradiction and, of course, the money that would be required for their services, Schoenberg and Stravinsky were both enticed to Hollywood (1934 and 1940 respectively), but neither composed a commercial film score. Only a handful of what can be considered as scores in a contemporary musical style were created in Hollywood during the pre-war years, most notably Aaron Copland's *Our Town* and *Of Mice and Men*, both from 1939, and Bernard Herrmann's *Citizen Kane* and *All That Money Can Buy*, both from 1941. The later earned Herrmann an Oscar, an award for a daring score that can be attributed, in part, to the unprecedented inclusion of film composers in the Oscar voting. Hanns Eisler was the first to adapt a twelve-tone technique for his score to *Hangmen Also Die!* (1943), but the length of music in the film is minimal, and the war placed a moratorium on such adventurous scoring.

As the tide of the war shifted towards the Allies in 1944, debates over the lack of contemporary musical qualities in Hollywood film music rekindled. A 1945 "Seminar of Music" at the Beverly Hills Hotel focused on the issue of modern music in film. Sponsored by the Hollywood Writers Mobilization, the panel was an unprecedented gathering of music educators—musicologist Dr. Walter Rubsamen, who would later serve as the chairman of the music department at UCLA, and Ingolf Dahl, a composer on the teaching staff of USC—and active film composers—Leigh Harline, Adolph Deutsch, and Hugo Friedhofer. Among others, David Raksin and UCLA musicologist Robert Nelson were vocal participants.[17] The session began with various definitions of modern music in film, and discussions centered on three issues: dissonance, color, and economy.

Dr. Rubsamen expressed a prevalent attitude:

> If a man is a gangster or somebody is being shot, then a contemporary dissonant idiom is okay, otherwise it has to be quite different. It has to be Tchaikovsky. Contemporary idiom and dissonance are associated with something evil on the screen. This points to one thing;

we have focused our attention too much on a negative definition of contemporary. There is a lack of appreciation of contemporary idiom and what it contributes to films.[18]

Rubsamen's impromptu comments touch on several associations that were common at the time. He describes conventional musical language with one word: "Tchaikovsky." That name, along with Rachmaninoff or simply "schmaltz," was equated with an old-fashioned romantic style out of step with modern tastes. Rubsamen follows this generalization by linking two concepts. Initially he refers to a "contemporary dissonant idiom," and shortly thereafter to a "contemporary idiom and dissonance." The word dissonance is dropped thereafter, but it is clear that, for Rubsamen and others, a contemporary idiom in film music had to include dissonance.

In retrospect, Hollywood composers did employ a substantial amount of dissonance during the Golden Age. Rubsamen aptly notes that dissonances would be used if someone is getting shot or to represent evil, and such moments can be quite extended, especially in action, adventure, and horror films. By the mid-1940s, Hollywood film music already contains many examples of sophisticated and occasionally radical harmonic treatment, given the right dramatic circumstances. Hence the primary goal in the second half of the decade was to expand the dramatic situations that could be underscored with dissonances.

During this time, color was an area of strength for Hollywood composers. Indeed, many had resources that extended beyond what a concert composer might expect with a symphony orchestra. A large studio orchestra had access to voices, to instruments associated with popular music, such as a vibraphone, and to newly developed electronic instruments, such as the Novachord, Hammond organ, and the theremin. With these tools, Rózsa and others explored combinations of color that were not heard in concert halls. In addition, studio orchestras played for microphones, which allowed for the hand of an engineer to alter, add, or mix sounds. Examples of such manipulations include the warbling piano in Raksin's score to *Laura* (1944), the eerie electronic buzz of telegraph wires in Herrmann's music for *All That Money Can Buy* (1941), and the layered effect of combining diegetic and non-diegetic music in Riesenfeld's remarkable score for *Sunrise* (1928).

In an article from 1946, Robert Nelson divides music into two types: color (the sensuous and exotic side of music) and line (the intellectual side of music).[19] Drawing this terminology from the debates in art history that centered on the paintings of Rubens (color and sensuality) and Poussin (line, clarity, logic, and order), Nelson argues that Hollywood film music is dominated by color. Among the most common types of color are imitations of ethnic styles, electronic instruments, and harmonic devices such as static harmony, ambiguity of key, parallelism, and complex chords, all areas well explored by Rózsa. Within the article, he describes numerous examples of what could be considered musical scores in a contemporary style, including Rózsa's music for *The Lost Weekend*.

While it might be argued that Hollywood composers were already incorporating modern harmonies and colors, the other element of contemporary music—economy and simplicity—was seen as a major weakness. Every panel member at the Music Seminar addressed the need for greater economy in film music, both in expressing emotions and in scoring. Friedhofer described a contemporary idiom: "We have simplicity, directness of approach, a complete avoidance of any of the technical procedures of the era immediately preceding ours." Harline spoke of an "economy of means and directness with which a specific emotion or feeling can be given to a musical notation," and Deutsch provides a clear manifesto for neo-Classicism in film music.[20]

In this area, film music in Europe was viewed as superior to that in Hollywood. At the 1951 International Music Congress in Florence, harsh criticisms for the lack of economy were leveled at specific Hollywood scores, including Rózsa's *Brute Force* and *A Double Life*. The economy of orchestration in Yves Budrier's music for *Les Maudits* was cited as a model of scoring. American critic Lawrence Morton responded: "But the larger issue of how and when to be economical appears to have been dodged. One would like to know, for instance, whether Baudrier's economy was dictated by aesthetic considerations or by a small budget, whether or not he had to underscore any earthquakes, chases, battles, or horse races."[21] Morton touches upon the essential issues concerning the lack of simplicity in Hollywood scoring, the needs of the films and the dictates of the studios. Even with the general movement towards greater musical economy in Hollywood during the late 1940s, it is unclear as to whether this is a result of the composers having more autonomy or of the financial decline of the studios.

Rózsa and Modern Music

Rózsa came to Hollywood just as these debates began to ferment. In 1946, he echoed many of the sentiments voiced at the Hollywood

"Seminar of Music" in an article written for the *Music Educators Journal*. After describing Hollywood film music of the last thirty years as being "post-Tchaikovsky and Rachmaninoff styles of yesterday," he concludes:

> Music in films reaches a greater audience than a composer could ever have dreamed fifty years ago. Its educational value is greater than that of concerts, radio or records. The musically ignorant man receives it subconsciously in the picture-show, and it becomes imperceptibly an actual part of his musical education. Here the film-composer bears the responsibility for forming the musical taste of a new generation.[22]

The question of how to write in a contemporary style within the Hollywood environment, of course, was another matter. Like many of his colleagues in the Hollywood coterie, Rózsa blamed the lack of a contemporary idiom in Hollywood film music on the studios. *Double Life* relates numerous instances of studio interference. Perhaps the most revealing conflict concerns the opening music for *Double Indemnity* (1944):

> The Music Director ... made no secret of the fact that he disliked the music intensely.... He reprimanded me for writing "Carnegie Hall" music, which had no place in a film. This I took as a compliment, but he assured me that it wasn't intended as such. He suggested that I should listen to Herbert Stothart's recent score to *Madame Curie* to learn how to write properly for the movies and, when I pointed out that the film was basically a love story, he described my title music to *Double Indemnity* as being more appropriate to *The Battle of Russia*.[23]

The title music for *Double Indemnity* is Rózsa's first major step towards expanding the role of dissonance. Significantly, Louis Lipstone (the music director in the above anecdote) did not directly object to the dissonances, but to their use outside of the context of a battle (or as Rubsamen described it, "someone being shot"). The burgeoning film noir genre provided a vehicle for composers to expand the use of dissonant harmonies. The sound of horror films could now underscore the gritty realism of America's darker side. Rózsa would be a leading figure in this trend, but he soon discovered that harsh dissonances and innovative colors were no longer considered to be modern by neo-Classic oriented critics. Achieving musical economy was difficult within the studio system, so Rózsa first explored a more stringent style in his concert music, which was then carried over into several of his scores from the late 1940s and early 1950s (see chapter 2).

Concert Music of the 1940s

Throughout his double life, Rózsa successfully revised excerpts from film scores for use as concert pieces. The most celebrated of these works is *Jungle Book Suite*. Modeled after Prokofiev's *Peter and the Wolf* (1936), the suite includes a narrator, associates animals with musical themes, and relates an abbreviated version of the classic story. Also achieving some prominence in the 1940s is the *Spellbound* Piano Concerto. This one-movement work has an ABA form in which the passionate love theme serves as the outer frames, while the B section presents a succession of other material from the film. Rózsa's romantic theatricality yields several climactic moments in the grand style of Rachmaninoff. Leonard Pennario performed the concerto and made the first recording.

The unabashed romanticism of the *Spellbound* Concerto contrasts substantially with the modernism of the Concerto for String Orchestra, Opus 17 (1943). This work shares a number of features in common with Ernest Bloch's Concerto Grosso No. 1 for Strings and Piano (1925), including fugal textures, parallel chords, and impressionistic colors. Rózsa pays homage to the Swiss/American composer with a reference to the opening measures of Bloch's work at his final cadence. Steven Wescott detects a sense of anger in Rózsa's concerto, which certainly has its counterpart in the film noir scores. He also notes its fine craftsmanship: "Whatever the source of the work's anger, it is nonetheless a stunning example of Rózsa's untarnished prowess as a composer. Many consider it among his best-crafted and most exciting compositions for the concert stage."[24]

In the late 1940s, Rózsa delved deeper into modernism. He described two of his neo-Classic concert works: "In 1948, a new style began to appear in my Piano Sonata—more percussive, contrapuntal, aggressive. The String Quartet continued this vein. Maybe it was an inner protest against the excessive amount of conventional music I had to write for conventional pictures."[25] Wescott describes the piano sonata as a "work of virtuosic dimension, conceding nothing for the sake of public taste or approbation. It is purposeful and demanding music, reminiscent of Bartók's assertive and unapologetically percussive writing for piano."[26] As in the neo-Classic works of Stravinsky, the sonata reflects qualities of the early classic or late baroque eras with its three-movement format and two-part invention texture for the first movement. The thematic material is stern, and the neo-tonal harmonies include extended triads and quartal chords. Periodically, overt folk qualities surface as well.

The string quartet, with four movements, is close in spirit to late Beethoven and Bartók. Most notable are the nationalistic features, which include pentatonic themes, dance rhythms with alternating metric patterns, and gypsy-like flourishes. Elliott W. Galkin reviewed the work in 1958: "This is a virtuoso quartet written by a composer who has a first-class knowledge of instrumentation. Although the piece hardly pioneers, it is vigorous, contemporary in idiom, filled with virtuoso stuff that 'sounds,' and merits performance by first rank string quartets."[27] The description "hardly pioneers" serves as a reminder that Rózsa was embracing a more "contemporary" sound just as the avant-garde was reinterpreting the concept of modern music.

Neo-Romanticism

The definition of neo-Romanticism, like those for modernism and neo-Classicism, is vague and subject to varied interpretations. Walter Simmons applies the term broadly to incorporate diverse musical figures such as Prokofiev, Vaughan Williams, Honegger, Bloch, and Howard Hanson.[28] Noting that the compositions of neo-Romantics are sometimes described as "movie" music, Simmons also considers Hollywood composers, including Steiner, Korngold, and Rózsa, to be neo-Romantics. One can view neo-Romanticism as a counterbalance to neo-Classicism. Both are products of the neo-tonal era, but the former retains ties to the gestures and emotional content of the nineteenth century, elements that are rejected by neo-Classicists. In this broad sense, Rózsa's Hungarian nationalism would be considered as a type of neo-Romanticism. In the context of this overview, however, I have reserved the term for Rózsa's works beginning in the 1950s in order to emphasize the sense of a romantic renewal in these compositions.

Rózsa's exploration of neo-Classicism continued into the early 1950s. But several factors led Rózsa to seek a balance between his modern and romantic musical personalities. In his film music, the decision by MGM to embrace features such as color, widescreens, and full symphonic scores encouraged Rózsa to incorporate some of the newer techniques, including harsh dissonances and counterpoint, into a romantic conception that would appeal to moviegoing audiences. In his concert music, Rózsa simply rejected the new aesthetics of the avant-garde and put a priority on the general listener:

> I do write my music for people, not for computers.... I believe in music as a form of communication; for me it is more an expression of emotion than an intellectual or cerebral crossword puzzle.... I find myself as out of sympathy with the so-called avant-garde of today as I did with the avant-garde of my own youth—Schoenberg and the Second Viennese School. I am an unashamed champion of tonality.[29]

Rózsa's neo-Romantic style is evident in his Violin Concerto, Opus 24,[30] premiered by Jascha Heifetz in 1953. Robin Holloway compares this work with the Korngold Violin Concerto: "Rozsa's Violin Concerto is in the same general area; as well crafted, and much leaner in texture. He builds better than Korngold (though both works reveal difficulty in reaching a punctual conclusion); the violinistic virtuosity is better integrated into the structure; and the slow movement achieves real melodic sweep. Rozsa's accent is, naturally, Hungarian, with Bartók behind and Kodály to the fore."[31] Bartók is not too far in the rear, as his colorful instrumentation, driving energy, and folk thematic material are invoked in all three movements. The aggressiveness of the string quartet is still evident, but it is softened by the lyric sweep. Writing music for such a public medium and for the greatest violinist of the era necessitated a return to a romantic conception, and it resulted in some of his most highly regarded works. Christopher Palmer has described the violin concerto as "arguably Rózsa's best work."[32]

Concert Music After 1960

When the contract with MGM expired in 1962, Rózsa began to produce concert works at a more consistent pace. *Notturno Ungherese* is Rózsa's last published work to make a direct reference to Hungary. It is a relatively brief single movement in an ABA structure. Nationalistic qualities—pentatonic flourishes and Scottish snaps—are most evident in the B section. The masterful craftsmanship of *Ben-Hur* is apparent in the orchestration, predominant lyricism, and varied harmony. Rózsa's keen sense of drama governs a careful buildup from a quiet opening to a satisfying climax. *Notturno Ungherese* is one of Rózsa's most attractive and finely crafted concert works.

During the next fifteen years, Rózsa would compose four major solo/orchestral works that would be premiered by some of the world's greatest performers: Sinfonia Concertante, Opus 29 (1966, Heifetz and Gregor Piatigorsky), Piano Concerto, Opus 31 (1968, Leonard Pennario), Cello Concerto, Opus 32 (1968, János Starker), and Viola Concerto, Opus 37 (1979, Pinchas Zukerman). These performances would bring considerable attention and acclaim to the composer. Other than the four-movement viola concerto, they retain the standard classical structural features of the concerto genre. All are built through elements of his nationalist techniques, although the amount of overt Hungarianness varies. The Viola Concerto, which Rózsa described as the last of "my little family of concerti for stringed instruments,"[33] is also his last large work, as he devoted himself to chamber works in the 1980s. His last published work is the Sonatina for Ondes Martinot, Opus 45 (1989).

By visualizing a double life, Rózsa could distance himself from the film composer that, by the definitions of modernist critics, was not creating significant music. He saw himself as a composer for the concert hall and justifiably took pride in his nonfilm works, which received regular publication and performances. But this repertory would never satisfy critics completely. Although his compositions for the concert hall received many positive reviews, the following comments on his Cello Concerto represent a prevalent attitude: "The musical idiom contains little that is novel.... Harmonically the work will no doubt be found more than a little démodé: the juxtaposition or superposition of unrelated triads, frequent parallelism, and plentiful ostinato patterns constitute the chief resources."[34] Critic Terry Teachout describes Rózsa's historical position:

> Rózsa paid a price for his worldly success. Although his concert music was admired and performed by distinguished artists like the violinist Jascha Heifetz, the cellist Gregor Piatigorsky, and the conductors Pierre Monteux and Bruno Walter, it was taken for granted by the vast majority of classical-music critics that a composer who wrote for Hollywood could not possibly be first-rate. There was an additional impediment to critical success: Rózsa refused to bow to postwar fashion and other avant-garde techniques. As a result, he became an increasingly marginalized figure.[35]

With historical perspective, the differences between Rózsa's two lives are less pronounced than one might assume from his autobiography and some of his other writings. His film music was on the contemporary edge, and his concert music was conservative. Both were challenged by Rózsa's desire to be viewed as a modern composer, and both ultimately rejected avant-garde attitudes and embraced neo-Romanticism. In a private interview, Rózsa acknowledged the similarity of his approaches to both mediums: "[Honegger's film music] style was the same as his style of concert music, and I think I inherited this from him; that I wrote serious music for films, just as I did for my concert music."[36] As he did throughout his career, Rózsa forged a synthesis of his two lives, and this resulted in memorable music for both the concert hall and movie theater, culminating with *Ben-Hur*.

2

RÓZSA'S TECHNIQUE OF FILM SCORING

Rózsa composed nearly one hundred original scores for narrative films. Within this output, one can hear a variety of approaches and techniques that result from the diverse needs of film genres, the tastes of directors and studios, and Rózsa's personal development and creativity. The divisions of his career into three periods detailed in chapter 1 coincide with changes in film assignments; the second period is dominated by film noirs, and the third centers on historical/action films.[1] But regardless of the evident diversity between individual films, genres, and stylistic phases, Rózsa maintained a certain consistency that he proudly called "Rózsaesque," elements of which are apparent in his earliest efforts.

The Early Films

In describing the experience of becoming reacquainted with his 1927 String Trio, Opus 1, Rózsa recalls: "I could see elements of immaturity, of course, moments when I was still feeling my way; but the basic characteristics of my mature style are, in embryonic formations, unmistakably present already."[2] In many ways, the same statement could be made about Rózsa's first film scores. There are novice mistakes to which he readily admits, but numerous compositional techniques are evident that will remain consistent throughout his career.

Among his strokes of good fortune must be counted the opportunity to compose for a variety of film genres in both London and Hollywood, most of which required moderate to full-length scores (Table

25

2.1). In these works, Rózsa quickly assimilated standard film-scoring gestures that would remain with him throughout his career, including rising sequences for tension, syncopated dissonant chords for action, lyric string writing for romance, and sprightly woodwind solos (typically a bassoon) for humor.

Although his earliest scores are written in London, they do not reflect a British influence, other than the approach to leitmotifs discussed below. Alexander Korda's studio emulated the style of Hollywood movies, hoping for greater financial rewards. Swynnoe notably regrets that Rózsa "never had the opportunity to score a good British film that was free of some form of internationalism."[3] Hence, Rózsa became familiar with the Hollywood musical style in England, and he continued to assimilate conventions of Hollywood's Golden Age after he arrived in America. In this process, Rózsa also developed his own distinctive voice. Although a novice to film, he had published about twenty concert works in the decade prior to 1937. For Rózsa, film music was simply a matter of adapting his Hungarian nationalist style to the needs of cinema.

Table 2.1. Rózsa's Scores for Narrative Films 1937-1943

Film	Year	Location	Genre	Scoring
Thunder in the City	1937	London	Comedy	Sparse
Knight Without Armour	1937	London	Adventure	Moderate
The Squeaker	1937	London	Crime	Moderate
The Green Cockatoo	1937	London	Crime	Moderate
The Divorce of Lady X	1938	London	Comedy	Moderate
The Four Feathers	1939	London	Adventure	Moderate
The Spy in Black	1939	London	War	Sparse
On the Night of the Fire	1939	London	Crime	Sparse
Ten Days in Paris	1940	London	Drama	Unavailable
The Thief of Bagdad	1940	London	Fantasy	Full
That Hamilton Woman	1941	London	Drama	Moderate
New Wine	1941	Hollywood	Biopic	Full
Lydia	1941	Hollywood	Drama	Moderate
Sundown	1941	Hollywood	War	Moderate
To Be or Not to Be	1942	Hollywood	Comedy	Sparse
Jungle Book	1942	Hollywood	Fantasy	Full
Five Graves to Cairo	1943	Hollywood	War	Full
So Proudly We Hail!	1943	Hollywood	Action	Moderate
Sahara	1943	Hollywood	War	Moderate
The Woman of the Town	1943	Hollywood	Western	Moderate

Melody

Rózsa's thematic material can be divided into three basic types: motivic, lyric, and ethnic. Motivic themes generally begin with a three to six-note unit that encompasses a modest range and draws its pitches primarily from a pentatonic scale. After its initial statement, this motive can be heard independently, possibly becoming a signifier of a person in the film, or it can be combined with other thematic ideas in order to build more extended melodies. The motive is frequently developed in subsequent passages, which may reflect onscreen situations. One typical alteration is the substitution of a tritone for a perfect fourth or fifth when there is danger.

Rózsa commonly builds his themes around the "cell" motive described in chapter 1—three central pitches that form the intervals of a major second and either a perfect fourth or fifth (Examples 1.1 and 1.2). This simple formula can generate a wide variety of themes (marked with brackets in Example 2.1). *The Squeaker* (2.1a) opens with a clear example of the motive. After its initial presentation, the idea alternates with other material and is subject to modifications. Elaborations on similar three-note ideas can be found in Rózsa's two most prestigious London scores. The title theme from *The Four Feathers* (2.1b) expands the length of the three-pitch motive with simple repetition, and, in *Knight Without Armour* (2.1c), the first measure defines the three principal pitches (B, E, D), and the second measure adds a C as a passing tone. Both of these motives undergo several variations during their narratives and eventually become embryos for love themes. While these first three examples encompass the range of a fourth, the theme from *The Spy in Black* (2.1d) inverts the perfect interval to a descending fifth, A-D-E. As such, its pitch content is identical to the first chord of *Ben-Hur*.

Example 2.1a. *The Squeaker.*

2.1b. *The Four Feathers.*

2.1c. *Knight Without Armour.*

2.1d. *The Spy in Black.*

2.1e. *That Lady Hamilton.*

2.1f. *The Green Cockatoo.*

2.1g. *Lydia.*

More elaborate variations on the cell motive can be seen in the next three examples. The inclusion of a tritone instead of a perfect fifth in the opening motive for *That Hamilton Woman* (2.1e) is unusual. Normally, Rózsa uses tritones to represent either an evil persona (such as Jaffar in *The Thief of Bagdad*) or a desperate situation for a leading character within the narrative. In this case, the dramatic opening statement underscores Emma's state at the beginning of the film, where she is in a pauper's prison. The title theme of *The Green Cockatoo* (2.1f), initially played by a clarinet, contains two adjacent three-note motives. The first extends for three beats and has a passing C; the second ascends and then falls to a cadence. The four principal pitches of these two measures (B, D, E, G) are members of a pentatonic scale. Similarly, the opening melody from *Lydia* (2.1g) contains two three-note motives that share a common pitch. The first four notes descend from B to F-sharp, and this last pitch initiates the second motive, a diminution of the first expanded to a fifth. This second idea returns at the end of the third measure.

Rózsa's ability to generate new material from motives is exemplified in the following excerpts from *Five Graves to Cairo*. The first measure of the title theme (Example 2.2a) presents a three-note motive (G, F, D) with a passing E-flat. The second measure is an elaboration of the first. Within the opening credits, this idea is transformed into a stirring march, and succeeding statements alter the intervals freely. During the desert trek scene, for example, the initial descent becomes a major third, and the next is a tritone (Example 2.2b). The use of chromaticism and tritones are also prominent in Ben-Hur's desert march. Later in the film, the head motive is transformed into a lyric love theme (Example 2.2c).

Example 2.2a. *Five Graves to Cairo*, **Title Theme.**

Example 2.2b. *Five Graves to Cairo*, **Desert Trek.**

Example 2.2c. *Five Graves to Cairo*, **Love.**

Rózsa's love themes, even when derived from germinal motives, stand apart from the other material and provide refreshing contrasts. Typically, they are lyrical and have balanced phrase lengths, expanded ranges, lush orchestration, and triadic harmonies. The melody of Example 2.2c immediately extends the range via an octave displacement, and it contains several gestures that surge both upward and downwards. For the most part, Rózsa's love themes move with conjunct motion, but they also generally contain one or more expressive leaps.

The love theme from *So Proudly We Hail!* (Example 2.3) begins with two measures centering on a cell motive (F-sharp, A, B). The last note is placed an octave lower to create a descending leap of a minor seventh and set up a surging rise and expansion of the range through measure four. The incorporation of triplets into the lyric flow and the chromatic inflection (B-flat) are also common characteristics. In their most typical presentation, love themes are played fully in the upper strings, while the French horn or cellos provide echo imitations, much in the tradition of Tara's theme from *Gone With the Wind*. In more intimate moments, a solo violin or cello will present the theme, often with more than a touch of saccharine.

Example 2.3. *So Proudly We Hail!*

Other than the biopic of Schubert (*New Wine*), *That Hamilton Woman* is the only historical setting in Rózsa's earliest films. The others are set either in the late nineteenth or twentieth centuries. The lack of variety in time is more than compensated with a range of locations that stretches across four continents. Source music typically signifies locations, such as the pub and street music in London scenes, the songs of Nazi or Russian revolutionaries, and a brass band rendition of "Aloha 'Oe" when Hawaii is the announced destination during *So Proudly We Hail!*. Rózsa's diegetic musical highlight in these early films is his use of an authentic Sudanese boating song performed with an antiphonal choir and drums in *The Four Feathers*.

Rózsa frequently incorporates specific tunes or regional styles in his score as well. These can be as simple as quoting "Russian Sailors Dance" or "God Save the Tsar" to delineate the combatants in *Knight Without Amour* and "La Marseillaise" and "Rule, Britannia!" for similar purposes in *That Hamilton Woman*. Rózsa's musical adaptability is certainly evident in *The Woman of the Town*, in which he evokes a standard Hollywood cowboy sound for the West and a Gershwin-like cue for New York City.

More significant evocations of ethnic styles can be found in the films set in Africa or Asia. In these, Rózsa employs tuneful themes with limited ranges, modal and pentatonic pitch content, and the conventional augmented-second interval. Zia (Gene Tierney) is given an Arabian dance theme with an augmented second in *Sundown*, creating a sinuous quality that matches her appearance in rather provocative clothing. The extended cues for solo flute and drums are similar to the timbres of the harp and flute in the love scene for Ben-Hur and Esther. For both, the music hovers between ethnic source music and scoring; initially heard as the former, it clearly functions as the latter by the end of the cue.

Example 2.4. *Sahara*.

The augmented second interval is also prominent in numerous cues in *The Four Feathers*, particularly those showing Khalifa's army of dervishes and fuzzy wuzzies. The extended drumming during these sequences, as it does in *Sundown*, also suggests an ethnic source. A good example of Rózsa's ethnic themes is the leitmotif for Tamboul, a Sudanese soldier in *Sahara* (Example 2.4). Like many of his other themes, it relies on pentatonic pitches, but its ethnic quality is created by pitch repetition, simple quarter-note rhythms, colorful orchestration (bells, harp), and occasional parallel-fourth harmony.

For the most part, Rózsa does not use themes with consistent associations in his London and early Hollywood films, other than love themes. *The Thief of Bagdad* is Rózsa's first major score to establish clear links between characters and musical themes. From this point, Rózsa incorporates leitmotifs in a moderate number of films, most notably in *Jungle Book, That Lady Hamilton, Sundown,* and *Five Graves to Cairo.*

Harmony

Another stylistic feature found in Rózsa's concert and film music is his general reliance on neo-tonality.[4] Dominant-seventh chords are easily avoided because of the lack of a leading tone in his modal and pentatonic thematic material and because of his frequent use of parallel chords. In general, Rózsa uses triads and triadic-based chords and generates dissonances with unresolved nontriadic pitches, extended triads, polychords, and quartal chords.

Example 2.5. *Five Graves to Cairo.*

Examples of these harmonic practices can be found in *Five Graves to Cairo.* Three quartal chords (Example 2.5) precede the initial statement of the title theme of Example 2.2a. Typical of Rózsa's quartal-chord construction, the bass instruments play open fifths, while the upper instruments contain three pitches related by fourths; in the first chord, these are A, D, G. In its pitch content and spacing, this chord recalls the previously discussed harmony from *Theme, Variations and Finale* (Example 1.3), and the progression foreshadows the opening chords to *Ben-Hur* (Example 4.2a), especially with its parallel movement involving a stepwise descent and return. The similarity between these two openings extends to the entrance of a low-register thematic idea. Unlike the motive in *Ben-Hur* (Example 4.2b), this one dwells on a nonchordal pitch—F (Example 2.2a), thereby producing harmonic tension that is sustained for three measures before the resolution to a C-minor-seventh chord.

Two other harmonic techniques can be observed in the score to *Five Graves to Cairo*. When the theme appears as a march during the opening credits, it is harmonized with parallel triads, and Rózsa freely moves between major and minor sonorities without regard to traditional harmonic rules. The music for the first scene contains several extended chords. For the desert walk, Rózsa combines two triads, an F diminished-seventh and G major, which would be heard as a G-ninth chord. The five pitches of this sonority are soon followed with a six-note chord: C, E, G-sharp, B-flat, D, F-sharp. Despite the spelling with consecutive thirds, the interval between G-sharp and B-flat is enharmonically a major second. Hence the chord could be defined as a polychordal combination of two augmented triads beginning on C and B-flat.

Similar harmonic complications can be found in several scores. An imperfect quartal harmony appears in the opening of *The Thief of Bagdad* (Example 2.6): E-flat, A, D, G. This substitution of a tritone for one of the perfect fourths will become more common in later works.

Example 2.6. *The Thief of Bagdad.*

The most striking harmonies in *That Hamilton Woman* take place during the Battle of Trafalgar, where extended triads and polychords are frequent. Example 2.7 shows one of the latter, in which Rózsa combines a G-flat diminished seventh with an A-major triad. The resultant six-note chord includes dissonant clashes of two major-seventh intervals. Similar harmonic treatment can be found in the battle at sea in *Ben-Hur*.

Example 2.7. *That Hamilton Woman.*

Orchestration

Rózsa began his career in London without the assistance of an orchestrator. He was initially dismayed when he was forced to use an orchestrator in Hollywood because of the union contract. Rózsa discussed the subject with Steven Wescott: "The system is not very artistic, but it has it merits, because it gives more time for the composition. They don't give you more time to orchestrate and compose. But all the time I can compose, and write out everything in four staves, or three staves, or five staves, or sometimes even ten staves, before the whole score."[5]

Rózsa composed his scores with specific orchestrations already in mind; generally, orchestrators were not left with any significant decisions. Lawrence Morton compared the completeness of Rózsa's manuscripts with those of Copland and others: "Copland's sketches are so complete that no other musical personality has an opportunity to intrude itself upon his music. Equally complete are the sketches of Adolph Deutsch, Hugo Friedhofer, David Raksin, and Miklós Rózsa, to name but a few."[6] Beginning with *That Hamilton Woman*, Rózsa consistently worked with fellow Hungarian Eugene Zador until the latter's death in 1977. Rózsa praised Zador for his faithfulness to his ideas: "Later I found someone who was very good and observed my sketches very religiously and didn't change anything. He was a Hungarian composer named Eugene Zador."[7]

Orchestration is one of Rózsa's most consistent and effective areas of composition. Many of his techniques are adapted from prevailing Hollywood trends, as exemplified in the works of Max Steiner. Rózsa's reliance on strings to generate lyric and action passages is typical of film scoring at that time. While the bulk of the melodic material is given to violins, a number of cues feature cellos and violas, creating dark and rich timbres that form a link to the traditions of middle-European string writing. As in his concert works, Rózsa periodically features a solo violin or cello to express tenderness or sadness. Woodwinds are primarily treated as solo instruments and are used for contrasting color and expressions ranging from humor to sadness. The low register of the flute with light accompaniment suggests a burgeoning or tender love relationship. Brass instruments provide power for action sequences, and the French horn often contributes to the sweep of passionate melodies.

Rózsa spices these standard orchestrations with some colorful moments. In *Knight Without Armour*, Rózsa highlights the bleakness of Siberia with stagnant harmonies and woodwind flutter tonguing, and the noirlike confession in *The Squeaker* features sul ponticello tremolos, harp, and bells. Rózsa employed similar colorful moments in his concert works. But in working with studio orchestras, he gained access to a new timbre not found in standard symphony orchestras—the wavering of the vibraphone and electric organ. He immediately exploited the sound in *Knight Without Armour* to suggest the madness of the train station porter, along with bells, tambourine, and piano. Cues featuring a vibraphone or an electric organ can also be heard in *The Green Cockatoo*, *The Thief of Bagdad*, and *Five Graves to Cairo*.

Rózsa's fascination with the wavering sound led to a thwarted effort to use the Ondes Martenot in *The Thief of Bagdad*. His first attempt to write for a theremin in *Sundown* was also unsuccessful. In its place, he used a musical saw to double choral humming accompanied by incessant drumming for the habari, an eerie night scene in which the natives wait for the curse of death to befall one of the European men.

Set Pieces

In addition to specific compositional techniques, Rózsa brought a symphonic conception into his film music. Given a lengthy cue and an appropriate scene (such as a montage), Rózsa crafted musical passages that could be transferred easily to the concert hall. The title music for *The Green Cockatoo* exemplifies this symphonic approach. Following fugal entrances based on the head theme, the tempo accelerates and two new melodies are introduced, the second of which initially appears to be source music on the train and underlies conversation. The following montage of London is scored with both themes, and the majestic conclusion is more appropriate for a Hollywood ending rather than a London beginning. Similar passages in the early films, especially from *The Four Features*, suggest that Rózsa may well have had the intention of making orchestral suites from the music of some of his early film scores, just as he had advised Honegger.

One recurring type of independent music in Rózsa's scores is the march. Perhaps inspired by the dramatic energy of Honegger's marches in *Les Misérables*, Rózsa created numerous equivalents in his early films. Three are prominent in *Knight Without Armour*: the march to Siberia, the march of Russians going to war, and a brief march when the mob confronts the Countess Vladinoff (Marlene Dietrich). In *Four Features*, the armies of Kitchener and Khalifa march to distinctively different musical styles. Among the other prominent marches are the exotic procession of the princess in *The Thief of Bagdad* and the prisoner march in *Five Graves to Cairo*. Needless-to-say, marches remained an important element of Rozsa's film music through *El Cid* and into the 1970s.

Film Noir

Rózsa entered the film noir phase of his career in the mid-1940s. Two-thirds of his film scores between 1944 and 1948 can be considered as noirs. By 1950, he had written music for eighteen noir-related films, which includes two of his three Oscar-winning scores—*Spellbound* and *A Double Life*—and recipients of three additional Academy nominations—*Double Indemnity*, *The Lost Weekend*, and *The Killers*. During this time, Rózsa underwent a stylistic change that consciously sought a more contemporary sound, as described in chapter 1. Rózsa's turn towards modernism in his film music can be seen in two phases. Initially he expanded the use of dissonances and explored new colors. Towards the end of the decade, he adopted the more economical neo-Classic approach.

Numerous issues surrounding film noir are still debated in cinema studies, including whether the genre is strictly an American phenomenon, when it began, and what type of film should be considered as noir. If we were to acknowledge that noirlike qualities exist in films from England and France, then one could well contend that Rózsa had already composed music for several film noirs prior to 1944. In *British Film Noir Guide*, Michael F. Keaney argues for the recognition of English films as noirs dating back to 1937. He includes in his canon *The Green Cockatoo*, which he cites as possibly the first English noir, *On the Night of the Fire*, and *The Spy in Black*, all of which have scores by Rózsa. With such a broad definition, one wonders why *The Squeaker*, with its extended noirlike climax, was not included. In addition, other early films with Rózsa scores certainly have noir moments, most notably *Five Graves to Cairo* from 1943.

Most traditional histories of film noir, however, limit their discussions to American films beginning sometime between 1940 and 1944. In the latter year, several classic noirs appear, including *Double Indemnity*, Rózsa's first major contribution to the genre. The film noirs scored by Rózsa, with the exception of the Deanna Durbin musical/comedy vehicle *Lady on a Train*, can be divided into three general types: pure noir, psychological noir, and melodramatic noir (see Table 2.2).[8]

Table 2.2. Rózsa's Film Noirs

Title	Year	Noir Type
Double Indemnity	1944	Pure Noir
Dark Waters	1944	Melodrama
Lady on a Train	1945	Comedy
The Lost Weekend	1945	Psychological
Spellbound	1945	Psychological
The Strange Love of Martha Ivers	1946	Psychological
The Killers	1946	Pure Noir
The Macomber Affair	1947	Melodrama
Brute Force	1947	Pure Noir
The Red House	1947	Psychological
Desert Fury	1947	Melodrama
A Double Life	1947	Psychological
Secret Beyond the Door	1948	Psychological
The Naked City	1948	Melodrama
Kiss the Blood Off My Hands	1948	Melodrama
Criss Cross	1949	Pure Noir
The Bribe	1949	Melodrama
The Asphalt Jungle	1950	Pure Noir

Characteristics of pure noir include murder, overriding pessimism, and tragic endings. The bleakness of human existence is best expressed in the final line of *Brute Force*: "Nobody escapes. Nobody ever really escapes." Psychological noirs involve some type of madness or psychological disorder. Melodramatic noirs also present dark and often morally ambiguous situations, but will end happily, as do psychological noirs. Following the standard Hollywood script, these films will have good winning over evil, and boy getting girl (or in the case of *Spellbound*, girl getting boy).

Pure Noirs

Rózsa's most significant innovations took place in his scores for pure and psychological noirs. The pure noirs establish a darker and more intense sound through dissonances and color. These changes are especially evident in the scores for *Double Indemnity*, *The Killers*, and *Brute Force*, all of which open with unrelenting, loud, brassy, dissonant marches driven by an ostinato-like pulse.

Example 2.8. *Double Indemnity*.

The score for *Double Indemnity* begins with a three-pitch cell motive that replaces the perfect fifth with a tritone (Example 2.8). This dramatic statement is punctuated by a six-note polychord combining the pitches of the G-flat major and A-flat augmented triads. The ensuing march, set over a continuously pounding timpani figure, unfolds in an A-A-B-A form. The "A" is a seven-measure phrase, in which the sixth measure contains an intense major-seventh dissonance that resolves into an imperfect five-note quartal chord (A-flat, D, G, C, F) and ultimately to an A-flat second-inversion chord at the beginning of the next phrase. It is problematic to refer to this theme as being in F minor. Certainly the pitches of the melody are taken from a pure minor (Aeolian) scale, but there is not one F-minor triad in the supporting harmony. Rózsa maintains this bleakness for the duration of the film, often employing polychords and quartal chords. Mr. Dietrich's murder, for example, is marked with the combination of a B-flat major triad and a C-sharp diminished-seventh, which creates two major-seventh clashes.

Many of these same qualities are intensified in the scores for *The Killers* and *Brute Force*. The former is the best known of Rózsa's noir music, since the opening motive is identified with the popular *Dragnet* television series. Always heard in a low-register, the curt motive contains four notes; with the periodic tritone cadence, the theme outlines a diminished triad (Example 2.9).

Example 2.9. *The Killers*.

The motive, a leitmotif for the killers, is one of three primary thematic ideas in the titles. The second is a series of harsh, syncopated polychords with roots separated by a tritone, a harmonic device that will be found in *Ben-Hur*. The third is an extended disjunct melody set over ostinato-like repetitions of the opening motive. It centers on a major-seventh leap, and continues with dotted rhythms and an unpredictable chromatic descent. The theme lends itself to imitation, and a two-part contrapuntal passage ensues, mirroring the pursuit of two killers. Critic John B. Currie notes: "The entire opening scene of the film is brilliant. There is a union, and integration of music and drama such as Hollywood seldom achieves."[9] Similar material, including violent syncopated dissonances (polychords and imperfect quartal chords) and disjunct melodic material, underscores the titles for *Brute Force*.

The effect of Rózsa's new sound is due not only to the harshness of the dissonances, but also to the darkness of the orchestration. Low and middle register brass instruments dominate more often than trumpets. The cellos and violas frequently carry the principal string melodies, and the violins are often given material that is played on their darker G and D strings. Rózsa's preferred woodwinds have become the oboe and clarinet, and within certain scenes with dark lighting (particularly notable in *Double Indemnity*), the bass clarinet. The timpani also gains greater prominence as a driving rhythmic device and as a solo instrument, such as the moments prior to the climactic shooting of Steve and Anna in *Criss Cross*.

Psychological Noirs

Double Indemnity and *The Strange Love of Martha Ivers*, both starring Barbara Stanwyck, have parallel plots in which a man and woman shoot each other or themselves near the end. Yet, *The Strange Love of Martha Ivers* is not considered to be a pure noir, but as a psychological noir because of Martha's madness generated out of guilt and greed and the happy ending for the other pair of lovers. Musically, this rather jolting and somewhat disappointing ending is foreshadowed in the opening credits with a soaring love theme. This melody, known as "Strange Love," became one of Rózsa's most popular.[10]

Like the stories themselves, the music for psychological noirs retains many of the qualities found in pure noirs. The two most distinctive differences characterizing the psychological type are the greater emphasis on love themes, such as "Strange Love," and the colorful wavering sounds used to suggest madness. These elements are readily evident in the score for Rózsa's best-known psychological noir, *Spellbound*. The music for the opening credits is typical of the psychological noir. Although it takes a major step towards modernism with its opening harmony and timbre (theremin), the modern passage is brief and immediately washed away with an extended love theme. The audience is immediately assured that, while there are disturbing events in the film, love will conquer all. There is no such message in the march for *Double Indemnity*.

The *Spellbound* love theme became Rózsa's most popular melody (Example 2.10a). The theme builds upon the qualities found in his earlier love themes, particularly in its expansive range and its *Gone With the Wind*-like sweep heard during the titles. Despite its grandeur, the elements of the theme are still drawn from Hungarian nationalism. The pitches, other than several passing notes and the expressive B-natural in the second measure, form a pentatonic scale (B-flat, C, E-flat, F, G). The third measure is similar to the first, as it inverts the downward leap to a B-flat to an ascent. In this measure, we can see the cell motive prevalent in Rózsa's earlier film scores most clearly.

Example 2.10a. *Spellbound,* **Love.**

Example 2.10b. *Spellbound,* **Madness.**

Rózsa employs the theremin in order to suggest moments of psychological instability for John Ballantine (Gregory Peck). This is not the first use of the instrument in a Hollywood film score,[11] but Rózsa brought the theremin to the public's attention with its prominent placement (beginning of the film) and its solo melodic material. In *Spellbound*, the theremin plays a distorted variation of the love theme (Example 2.10b). The rhythms and contour of the first four pitches for both are nearly identical, and the cadence of the madness theme, as in the love theme, is a variation of its opening gesture. Descending chromatic pitches and a tritone interval (G-natural to C-sharp) suggest John's disorientation, a quality that is supported by the stagnant and dissonant harmonies.

Rózsa used the theremin in two additional films. For Best Picture winner *The Lost Weekend*, the instrument underscores alcohol carvings.[12] The principal theremin melody is similar to its counterpart in *Spellbound*, with descending chromatic movement and tritones; the melody outlines a diminished seventh chord. In several dramatic moments, such as the desperation at the end of the pawnshop montage and the horror at seeing the wall oozing with blood, the theremin sustains just a single pitch while the orchestra plays thematic material. In *The Red House*, the theremin has colorful company, including the Novachord, vibraphone, and celesta. Once again the theremin often sustains single pitches while other instruments, including the vibraphone, play melodic material. In this way, the theremin suggests the mysterious screaming that Pete (Edward G. Robinson) describes. Later on, the theremin joins with the other wavering and bell-like instruments in the playing of an eerie nursery tune at the red house.

Wanting to avoid the overuse of the theremin, Rózsa did not employ the instrument in his other scores. He found alternate means to fill the role of a disturbing musical sound in his psychological noirs. For the Oscar-winning score to *A Double Life*, Rózsa employed Renaissance music to capture the dual personalities of Anthony John (Ronald Colman) as a real-life stage actor and as the imaginary and stage persona Othello. Two moments are particularly striking. In the first, Anthony is looking at a travel poster to Venice, and the harpsichord plays a stately Renaissance dance doubled by a vibraphone. In the second, Anthony is at a party watching a pianist playing popular music, but he is hearing the faint sounds of Venetian music in the style of Giovanni Gabrieli.

Also notable is the score for *Secret Beyond the Door*, which contains varied colors including those of a mandolin, guitar, Novachord, vibraphone, celesta, and string harmonics and sul ponticello. Rózsa describes an innovative technique that he used for the film: "Lang wanted an unusual sound and, since I refused to use the theremin again, we experimented with having the orchestra play their music backwards, recording it back to front on the tape, and then playing it back as usual; the end result sounded the right way around but had an unearthly quality."[13] The "unearthly effect" underscores Celia's discovery of the secret beyond the door—she is the next murder victim.

Rózsa stands as a central figure in the musical sound of film noir. Film and television composers assimilated the dissonance, dark orchestration, overall pessimistic mood, and wavering sounds into their scores for detective, horror, science fiction, and dramatic stories. Maintaining his leadership, Rózsa would also point to a new and more economical approach to scoring noirs, which coincides with the genre's move towards greater realism in the late 1940s.

Neo-Classic Tendencies (1948-1950)

Rózsa had created a dramatic new sound with his scores for film noirs, but it would have been difficult to sustain that intensity and distinctive timbre for any length of time without lapsing into parody. One can already hear weak echoes of *The Killers* in the music for *Criss Cross* (1949). Moreover, the scores for *Brute Force* and *A Double Life* were being criticized in Europe for their lack of economy. In response, Rózsa moved away from the brutal harshness of his early noir scores and began to embrace neo-Classicism. Lawrence Morton describes this shift in style:

> It is not an exaggeration to say that the large, sustained brass sonorities typical of the earlier scores are now being dissolved into their component parts and given linear configurations. This marks a shift from luxury of sound to muscularity, from static sonority to forward motion, from the eloquence of rhetoric to the eloquence of gesture. In part it answers the need, in film music, for a stricter and more formal logic than that provided by the Wagnerian symphonic style that has for so long dominated film music. It is perhaps not possible to find in Rozsa's music a consistent line of development in these matters. Like every film composer with a new idea, he has advanced cautiously, and with the limitations imposed by each film. But if one compares the *Spellbound* music with that for *Asphalt Jungle* it becomes immediately apparent that Rozsa has not stood still for six years. He is moving in the same direction as the more progressive of his colleagues. This is in every way a hopeful sign, and it could conceivably have the result of bringing film music more in line, stylistically, with the best trends in contemporary concert music.[14]

The term "transition" is admittedly overused, but it certainly seems appropriate for these scores. The years 1948-1950 are transitional to society as a whole—adjustments to postwar life and to the onset of the Cold War in a nuclear age—to the film industry—a rapid financial decline and attacks from HUAC—and to classical music—a quiet neo-Classic lull before the onset of the avant-garde. During these years, significant steps were taken in Hollywood film music towards the incorporation of more pronounced modernism, as evident in the works of David Raksin, Hugo Friedhofer, Bernard Herrmann, and the first scores from Alex North. Hollywood's acceptance of a more contemporary idiom are reflected in the Best Dramatic Score Oscar winners for 1948-1950: Brian Easdale's *The Red Shoes*, Aaron Copland's *The Heiress*, and Franz Waxman's *Sunset Boulevard*.

Rózsa's adoption of neo-Classic techniques can be seen in his more thorough integration of imitative and nonimitative counterpoint, greater reliance on dissonance, and more economical approach to orchestration, emotionalism, and the amount of music. A marked increase in contrapuntal activity is already evident in scores dating back to 1947, such as the lively Baroque fugue (with a bit of Venetian flavoring) heard just after the successful premier of *Othello* in *A Double Life*. Quasi-canons and fugal treatment also achieve prominence in *The Red House*, *The Macomber Affair* (suggesting hunting), *Kiss the Blood Off*

My Hands (suggesting a chase), and *Desert Fury*. Rózsa's search for simplicity and economy is best seen in *Crisis* (1950), which mimics the character of *The Third Man* with its extended use of a regional folk instrument—a solo guitar.

Several distinctive scores appeared in 1948. *A Woman's Vengeance* is based on an Aldous Huxley screenplay, an adaptation of the writer's own short story. Perhaps the literary connection suggested less conventional music; Rózsa responded with a sparse score that uses a small orchestral ensemble and contains numerous contrapuntal episodes and extended passages of dissonance. The most striking cue occurs just as Henry (Charles Boyer) discovers that his wife has died. Here Rózsa provides a chromatically saturated theme with ten different pitches within its first four measures (Example 2.11).

Example 2.11. *A Woman's Vengeance.*

Also from 1948, *Command Decision* has an economical score with several colorful and pervasive dissonant cues, most notably when Clark Gable ponders his command decisions while staring at a bombing map. Among its numerous harmonic complexities is a striking passage of parallel four-note quartal chords supporting the basic cell motive heard in earlier films (compare Examples 2.1 and 2.12), a harmonic sound that will be used with the Anno Domini theme in *Ben-Hur*.

Example 2.12. *Command Decision.*

Between 1948 and 1950 Rózsa provided music for four noirs: *The Naked City* (1948), *Criss Cross* (1949), *The Bribe* (1949), and *The Asphalt Jungle* (1950). The two from 1949 retain stylistic ties to earlier noirs, but also exhibit some of the newer tendencies, such as the two prominent fugues in *The Bribe*. The first, occurring just about forty minutes into the film, has a chromatic theme that recalls the first movement of Bartók's *Music for Strings, Percussion and Celesta*.

The Naked City and *The Asphalt Jungle* reflect the shift in film noir towards a more realistic and quasi-documentary style. As such, musical cues are minimal and generally dissonant. The climactic scene of *The Naked City* relies heavily on counterpoint and syncopated, dissonant chords for the dramatic action. With the epilogue, composed as a tribute for the sudden passing of the director Mark Hellinger, Rózsa turns to a warmer sound that features numerous rising repetitions of a three-note cell motive (Example 2.13).

Example 2.13. *The Naked City.*

Scoring for *The Asphalt Jungle* is limited to two cues (beginning and end). At the onset of the narrative, Rózsa employs three musical elements that recall Stravinsky's *Rite of Spring*—a sustained flute trill, sporadic double chords (two quick strokes, some of which have parallel fourths), and a strained bassoon timbre. A bassoon duet ensues that suggests the economical neo-Classic sound of Stravinsky's later works. The final cue returns to the stuttering syncopation of the opening, suggesting that Dix is once again being hunted. When he reaches his home ranch at the end of the film, the music becomes more expansive with a brief mimicking of Copland's American nationalist style.

During these transition years in which films such as *A Woman's Vengeance* and *The Asphalt Jungle* suggest growing modernism in Rózsa's film scoring, two of his scores from 1949—*The Red Danube* and *Madame Bovery*—retain traditional features. The former film features a variety of musical sounds, including traditional romantic cues, a heavy Russian theme, and one of Rózsa's simplest contrapuntal tasks, incorporating "Row, Row, Row Your Boat" into the score. Much more substantive is the score for the film based on a literary classic, *Madame Bovery*. With its passion, color, and sensational waltz, the music is considered to be Rózsa's best score from the late 1940s. Rózsa described the score as "romantic, luxurious and expressive,"[15] which clearly separates this work from his other film scores at this time. This is not the harbinger of a new film style but rather a reflection of romantic traditions that are appropriate for the nineteenth-century setting of the story.

Towards *Ben-Hur* and Beyond

Hollywood filmmaking underwent significant changes in the early 1950s, largely due to competition from television. Prior to 1951, Rózsa had supplied scores for only a half dozen color films, including the adventure drama *The Four Feathers*, two adventure fantasies, *The Thief of Bagdad* and *Jungle Book*, and two musical biopics, *A Song to Remember* and *Song of Scheherazade*. Beginning with *Quo Vadis* (1951), most of Rózsa's assignments would be for color films. In 1953, Rózsa composed the music for MGM's first film shot with Cinemascope, *Knights of the Round Table*, and for the first film to be recorded in four-track stereo, *Julius Caesar*.[16]

These technological innovations, along with colorful, sweeping scores, helped usher in Hollywood's blockbuster era. Working for MGM, Rózsa was one of the decade's most productive and highly regarded composers. Between 1951 and 1959, he composed twenty-six film scores; he received Academy nominations for *Quo Vadis*, *Ivanhoe*, and *Julius Caesar*, and won his last Oscar for *Ben-Hur*. Four trends can be observed in Rózsa's scores from this decade: the emergence of a neo-Romantic style, the use of popular musical themes, the expanded role of leitmotifs, and a more realistic depiction of time and place. All of these developments have a direct impact on the music for *Ben-Hur*.

Rózsa continued to use a neo-Classic style in several of his scores in the first half of the decade. The narrative for *Men of the Fighting Lady* (1954), for example, has only one cue, which extends nearly twenty minutes with unresolved dissonances. For the most part, though, Rózsa absorbed modernist elements into a romantic sweep that touched upon a broader range of emotions. The harmonic treatment of the film noir scores now heightened the emotional intensity of action sequences and moments of tragedy, and the techniques of Hungarian nationalism fashioned distinct ethnic and historical styles.

Theme songs with popular appeal have long been a staple of Hollywood music. Rózsa mentions it as a factor in his scoring in 1946: "Our first film was … *Strange Love of Martha Ivers*, for which I was told a 'theme song' was wanted. This was the fashion now, a tune to which lyrics could be added and broadcast as a 'plug' for the film."[17] With the commercial success of Dimitri Tiomkin's "Do Not Forsake Me, Oh My Darlin'" from *High Noon* in 1952, studio pressure for hit songs became even more pronounced. Rózsa responded with two choral themes in 1954, "Blind Flight," a stirring anthem for *Men of the Fighting Lady*, and an exotic theme for *Green Fire*. The latter is incor-

porated into the score, where it is more effective than the choral renditions that frame the film. A number of Rózsa's instrumental themes
also have a songlike character. One of his most attractive melodies
from the 1950s is the title theme for *Diane* (1956). Called "Beauty and
Grace," this was later arranged for strings and enjoyed moderate success in schools and concert halls. Although not a title theme, Esther's
theme from *Ben-Hur* fills the function of a popular lyric melody, and
some would consider it to be Rózsa's most beautiful instrumental
theme of the decade.

In general, Rózsa uses leitmotifs in a more consistent manner in
the 1950s than in his earlier films. Many of these identify the principal
characters of the story. Rózsa began to create stronger heroic themes
for the protagonists. Both *All the Brothers Were Valiant* (1953) and *Tip
on a Dead Jockey* (1957), for example, employ melodies that resemble
themes in *Ben-Hur*. Example 2.14 is similar to the Hatred theme (Example 4.6) without the tritone cadence, and 2.15 adumbrates the theme
for Ben-Hur (Example 4.4a).

Example 2.14. *All the Brothers Were Valiant.*

Example 2.15. *Tip on a Dead Jockey.*

Between 1944 and 1950, the majority of Rózsa's film assignments
were contemporary dramas in urban settings. This trend was reversed in
1951 with the epic *Quo Vadis*, set in Rome in the early years of the
Christian church. There followed a series of films set in numerous international locales and in a variety of historical periods ranging from
antiquity to the *fin de siècle*. For the most part, Rózsa skillfully crafted
scores that reflected the time and location of the plots while meeting
the demands of studios and American audiences, an ability that will
come to full fruition in *Ben-Hur*.

Bhowani Junction (1956) and *Something of Value* (1957) are two
of Rózsa's most thoroughly ethnic scores. The music for *Bhowani
Junction* includes ethnic drums, a sitar, an Indian flute, and various
combinations of western instruments that suggest an Indian ambiance.
African choral music is the primary musical sound for *Something of*

Value, set in Kenya. The singing of African texts (some cues are merely hummed) is either a cappella or accompanied with percussion. The melodic material is predominantly pentatonic, another variation of Rózsa's Hungarian nationalism. Western influences can be heard in the prevailing quadruple meter and the occasional harmony, such as with the Hollywood choral ending. Still, the overall effect suggests authenticity. Both of these films employ an extended low-register flute solo with minimal or no accompaniment, a scoring device that will recur in *Ben-Hur* and in other films with exotic settings. The cue in *Something of Value* is particularly colorful, as the alto flute is doubled with a vibraphone and musical saw while string harmonics, harp, piano and marimba sustain a quartal chord.

Historical styles are similarly assimilated into Rózsa's scores during this period, which Palmer suggests was a special strength for Rózsa:

> Rózsa sought out and studied what music was available and achieved a synthesis of elements of the older style within his personal idiom. This ability to express the past in music of the present is a rare gift. The success of Rózsa's historical music stems from the fact that he never tries to be artificially or self-consciously archaic, merely to be himself, musically speaking, at a variety of points in times past. He absorbs the spirit of a period style and then recreates his own musical personality within its frame of reference.[18]

Several films from the 1950s absorb Renaissance features in their scores, most notably *Plymouth Adventure* (1952) and *Diane* (1956). In the former, a story about the voyage of the Mayflower, Renaissance dances, the sound of a harpsichord, modal thematic material, and a recurring hymn suggest the late fifteenth-century time period. As noted by Palmer, Rózsa based the chorale on a setting of Psalm 136 in the 612 *Henry Ainsworth's Psalter*, which research had shown was used by the Pilgrims.

For *Diane*, Rózsa employs Renaissance cadential formulas as thematic material. One of the most striking moments is the music for the death of King Francis I. Here Rózsa combines the *Dies irae* (see the tenor voice in Example 2.16) with the tempo and rhythm of a funereal pavane. The upper register maintains a pedal E with a pavane rhythmic motive. The overall sound conjures up the A-minor second movement of Beethoven's Symphony No. 7 at the entrance of the countermelody.

Example 2.16. *Diane.*

The Path to *Ben-Hur*

In addition to the general trends discussed above, a handful of Rózsa's film scores lead more directly to *Ben-Hur*. The first and most obvious of these is *Quo Vadis*, Rózsa's first epic score and a major triumph for the composer. Lawrence Morton describes his initial response to the music: "I can remember no recent score from any studio in which the music has been quite so ear-filling without ever becoming ear-splitting." He later referred to it as "perhaps his most impressive score and certainly his most effective from a theatrical point of view."[19]

Like *Ben-Hur*, this film is a remake of a prominent silent film, and it combines a romance, in which a female converts her Roman lover to Christianity, and a Christian story, Peter's crucifixion. The filmmakers and Rózsa devoted much time toward authenticity. Replicas of Roman instruments are seen prominently in fanfares and parades. Going beyond instrumentation, Rózsa studied surviving fragments of Greco-Roman music and paraphrased a number of these melodic phrases in his score. Nero's newly composed song, for example, is derived from an ancient Greek melody known as the *Epitaph of Seikilos.*[20]

In his autobiography, Rózsa notes that he established his "Roman style" with this film.[21] For the most part, the Roman world is depicted through its source music. The magnificence of Rome is seen in the pageants, calling for numerous brass fanfares and two substantial marches. Imbedded within the first march is the heroic leitmotif of Marcus Vinicius (Robert Taylor). The low brass intones his theme during the middle portion of an ABA form, just as the Ben-Hur theme is heard in the trio of the "Parade of the Charioteers." Standard characteristics of the Roman marches include dotted rhythms, Scottish snaps, quick imitation, and emphatic pulses. Nero describes the total effect as "strong, brave, relentless." The second march of the film, "March of a New Era," reappears in *Ben-Hur* as "Circus March." Roman source music also includes exotic barbarian dancing, which suggests the decadence of the society. Keeping to the traditions of such scenes in epic films, Rózsa's dances are in frantic tempos, have syncopated rhythms, and feature prominent drums with woodwinds playing repetitive and limited-range melodic material. Suggestions of a monophonic texture and frequent parallel chords also imply savage, primitive music.

The underscoring for *Quo Vadis* is generally limited to moments of action and romance and to scenes of the Christian world. The film features a chariot race that foreshadows *Ben-Hur* with its visions of a whip and two wheels that tangle. Unlike the *Ben-Hur* race, this scene is accompanied by action music that includes fanfare material, a brass dominated timbre, and the Marcus Vinicius leitmotif. The love theme between Marcus Vinicius and Lygia is subtle, perhaps suggesting their ultimate subordination to the love for Christ. Much stronger in character is the love theme (with a dash of Spanish coloring) between Petronius and Eunice. Neither matches the passion and beauty of Esther's theme in *Ben-Hur*.

While the Roman music of *Quo Vadis* is similar to that in *Ben-Hur*, the Christian music differs substantially. In *Quo Vadis*, Rózsa relies more heavily on chantlike qualities, as several themes are based on Gregorian or other Christian chant. Still, some elements can be heard in common between the two films: Christian themes are modal and tend to have limited ranges; parallel triadic chords are employed, particularly with the mention of Christ; and prominent Christian moments are given special orchestrations. When Christ confronts Peter, a wordless choir enters accompanied by high strings. At the climax, the choir sings more fully with a text ending in Alleluia. The organ also makes a brief entrance at this moment.

Rózsa's only other score of a sword-and-sandal film prior to *Ben-Hur* is for *Julius Caesar* (1953) based on Shakespeare's play. The nature of this classic drama is far removed from *Quo Vadis*, as is evidenced by the black-and-white cinematography. The ghostly apparition scene even evokes a film noir-like atmosphere with its vibraphone/wordless choir timbre. Still, many of the source-music qualities from *Quo Vadis* resonate in *Julius Caesar*. Brass fanfares abound, often with Scottish snaps. Frequent imitative textures highlight the new stereo technology. Several marches are presented, one of which shows numerous cornus. A particularly stirring march is heard during the death scene of Brutus, in which the brass and woodwind march gets increasingly louder and closer (via stereo) as Marc Anthony approaches, and a string countermelody depicts Brutus's death. At the end, the march continues, "strong, brave, relentless."

Julius Caesar also has one unique use of source music: John Dowland's "Now, O now I needs must part" is sung for Brutus. This conscious musical reference to the age of Shakespeare rather than to antiquity recalls the mixture of the two worlds in Laurence Olivier's *Henry V* (1944). Rózsa admits employing this melody as an historical reference: "Shakespeare only indicates 'music and a song,' and I thought that an Elizabethan song, because of its language, would be the most appropriate. I chose John Dowland's 'Now, O now, I needs must part,' which was published in 1597 and might have been known to Shakespeare."[22]

As important as *Quo Vadis* is as a forerunner to *Ben-Hur*, certain musical qualities are developed more thoroughly in film scores for plots set in English history, particularly *Ivanhoe* (1952) and *The Knights of the Round Table* (1953). Roman-styled fanfares and marches are borrowed and placed into these later eras. John Fitzpatrick points out that the same fanfare is used in *Ivanhoe, Young Tess*, and *Ben-Hur*, hence bridging antiquity, medieval times, and the Renaissance.[23] In *Diane*, a story set in the sixteenth century, we are even shown Roman cornus during the lively procession of the Medici family.

Much of the score for *Ivanhoe* is derived from the fanfares and from Robert Taylor's opening rendition of a troubadour song. The interrelationship of themes, the clearly defined leitmotifs, and the excellent action cues serve as strong precedents for the *Ben-Hur* score. Rózsa also creates a significant new sound not found in *Quo Vadis*, a Jewish quality for Rebecca (Elizabeth Taylor). Her modal theme, generally played by strings in a lower register, has a strong pickup gesture, the basic range of a fifth, a quick ornamental turn, imitative accompaniment, and a passionate yearning quality (Example 2.17). Clearly the musical highlight of the score, this melody is a worthy predecessor of Esther's theme.

Example 2.17. *Ivanhoe*, **Rebecca Theme.**

In a similar fashion, the score for *The Knights of the Round Table* exhibits several *Ben-Hur* qualities. Evildoers are represented with dotted rhythms, parallel chords, and descending tritones. The action hero, Sir Lancelot, has an expansive theme resembling Ben-Hur's with its strong dotted rhythm and octave leap. Action sequences include trumpet battle calls and brief references to characters, similar to what is heard in the sea battle of *Ben-Hur*. In addition, the film develops an important Christian sound with the leitmotif for the Holy Grail. The theme itself is modal, has a limited range, and is supported with parallel triads shifting between major and minor sonorities. The timbre, with the wavering tones of an organ, string and harp harmonics, celesta, woodwinds, voices, vibraphone, and chimes, adumbrates the Christ sound of *Ben-Hur*, as detailed in chapters 4 and 5.

After *Ben-Hur*

Rózsa scored three more epic films in the years immediately following *Ben-Hur*: *El Cid* (1961), *King of Kings* (1961), and *Sodom and Gomorrah* (1962). Although the two biblical epics maintain the general style established in *Ben-Hur*, neither is as successful as their predecessor. In spite of an $8 million budget, 300 sets, and 20,000 extras, *King of Kings* is less monumental and less emotionally intense than *Ben-Hur*. *Sodom and Gomorrah*, Rózsa's only score for a biblical film based on a story from the Old Testament, has a wider range of emotions and several spectacular scenes, including an extended battle with fire and water and God's destruction of Sodom. Parallels to the plot in *Ben-Hur* include the focus on a personal story against the backdrop of a biblical event, a figure that is transformed into what he initially hates (Ben-Hur becomes a Roman, and Lot becomes a Sodomite), and a catharsis then helps the hero find a way back to his original self. Perhaps because of its subject, the music for *Sodom and Gomorrah* is more dissonant and assimilates Jewish folk and religious qualities more thoroughly than Rózsa's other religious scores. Unfortunately, the music does not rescue the film, as noted by Solomon: "In *Sodom and Gomorrah*, Rozsa's moving music has little real drama to accompany."[24]

Rózsa considered *El Cid* (1961) to be his last major film score, and it stands as a worthy counterpart to *Ben-Hur*. In preparation, Rózsa studied the *Cantigas de Santa Maria*, where he found numerous melodies and phrases that could be incorporated into his thematic material. Composing in Spain, he absorbed many of the regional traditions, and the score is enlivened with Spanish rhythms, dissonances, and melodic turns. With its spectacular battle scenes and intense love story, the film provides Rózsa with many opportunities to compose exciting and emotionally intense musical cues. His colorful musical palette includes the Spanish guitar, a dramatic solo organ for the final scene (reinforcing the religious implications), and harmonically clashing trumpet fanfares.

With the decline of the epic genre, Hollywood's changing attitudes towards film music, and his professional attention turning more towards concert music, Rózsa's film scoring became sporadic during his last two decades of activity. Rózsa received his final two Oscar nominations for *El Cid*, one for Best Score and one for Best Song. Formal recognitions of his later scores are limited to a César (Académie des Arts et Techniques du Cinéma in France) for *Providence* (1977) and a Saturn (Academy of Science Fiction, Fantasy & Horror Films in the U.S.) for *Time After Time* (1979).

None of the late film scores would match *El Cid* in quality, but examples of his artistry are ample, including the thematic material inspired by Sibelius's *Valse Triste* for *Fedora* (1978), the violin solos borrowed from his Violin Concerto for *The Private Life of Sherlock Holmes* (1970), and several beautiful love themes, such as in *The V.I.P.s* (1963) and *Last Embrace* (1979). Among the notable orchestration moments are the fountain scene in *The Golden Voyage of Sinbad* (1977), the harpsichord and recorder timbers for *The V.I.P.s*, and the cimbalom for *The Power* (1968). The later also contains some of his most dissonant harmonic treatment. For the Steve Martin film noir spoof *Dead Men Don't Wear Plaid* (1982), Rózsa brought his film career to a close with an appropriate mimicking of his own music from the 1940s.

3

THE HISTORICAL AND CRITICAL CONTEXT OF *BEN-HUR*

"My God, did I set all this in motion?"

Lew Wallace's astonishment after seeing the Broadway production based on his novel must have been genuine. In writing *Ben-Hur: A Tale of the Christ* (1880), he had no expectation that his third literary effort would become America's best selling novel, a position that it held for half a century before being surpassed by *Gone With the Wind* (1936). The popularity of *Ben-Hur* led to a long-running theater adaptation with spectacular effects, including an onstage chariot race, hundreds of extras, and music for voices and orchestra. One can only imagine what Wallace would have thought of later developments. He died of cancer in 1905 at the age of seventy-seven, just two years prior to the appearance of the first of four film versions of the story: an early silent film, an epic silent film, the 1959 MGM classic, and a made-for-television animation feature. In the view of Jon Solomon, the story of Ben-Hur was the "most dependable theatrical war horse of the century."[1]

Each rendition of the story required modifications reflecting the advantages and limitations of the given medium and the prevailing trends of the time. Aspects of each interpretation were assimilated in succeeding productions, and, in this manner, adaptations for the Broadway play can also be found in the later film versions. Among the connecting links is the prominent role of music for each version of the story. Hence, the Wyler film combines the essence of the original novel, aspects of each major interpretation, and unique elements reflecting its own era.

Popular and critical responses to the novel and the various adaptations have been consistent. *Ben-Hur* has enjoyed phenomenal popular acclaim, setting records as a novel, attendance figures as a play, and Oscars as a film. For all of these successes, critics have been divided. Some have echoed the public's reaction, but others have expressed harsh criticisms, often ridiculing the intelligence of those that enjoy the novel, play, or film. This split between popular and critical views has followed *Ben-Hur* and its various interpretations from the late nineteenth century into the twenty-first century.

The Novel

Lew Wallace

There are a number of parallels between the lives of Lew Wallace and that of Ben-Hur. Like the fictional character, Wallace was a modern day American prince. His father David Wallace was a political figure in their home state of Indiana; he served as governor, congressman, chairman of the Indiana Whig party, and a state judge until his death in 1859. Lew's stepmother Zerelda G. Wallace was also a public figure. A contemporary of Susan B. Anthony, she was a leader in both the temperance and suffrage movements. Before turning thirty, the young Wallace practiced law and was elected to the State Senate.

In the novel, Ben-Hur actively gathers soldiers in preparation for a war against Rome. This too is a reflection of Wallace's life, in which he twice raised militia companies. The first was for the Mexican-American War (1846-1848), in which the United States won the dispute over Texas and claimed the territories of California and New Mexico as well. Wallace did not serve in combat, but rose to the rank of first lieutenant in the army of future President Zachary Taylor. At the onset of the Civil War, Wallace again recruited troops in Indiana and eventually became a general, the youngest at that rank in the Union army.

Wallace generally distinguished himself in his military service, but was blamed for the early Union failures at the Battle of Shiloh. Wallace felt that Ulysses S. Grant used him as a scapegoat to cover his own inefficiencies. Military historian Victor Davis Hanson observes:

> The entire plot of *Ben-Hur: A Tale of the Christ* eerily resembles much of Wallace's own sad odyssey following that disaster of April 6, 1862. For all its subplots revolving around Christ, *Ben-Hur* is

mostly the saga of a young, brilliant Jewish hero whose adult life is devoted to seeking revenge for an injustice done him and his family—by no less than a friend who knew better and would benefit from his duplicity.[2]

Emotionally, Wallace never recovered fully from this perceived betrayal, but his political career did rebound. Because of his military and legal backgrounds, he was chosen to serve on the commission for the trial of the Lincoln assassination conspirators, and he presided over the court-martial of Henry Wirz, the commandant of the horrific Andersonville prison. Descriptions of the conditions and disease at this infamous Confederate camp are certainly reflected in the Valley of Lepers in *Ben-Hur*.

After the war, Wallace held several political posts in Indiana, was appointed governor of the New Mexico Territory, and became U.S. Minister to the Ottoman Empire. While serving in New Mexico, he offered amnesty to the famed outlaw Billy the Kid and reportedly completed the Crucifixion portion of his novel shortly after their meeting. David Mayer also suggests that the arid weather and multi-ethnic confluence encountered by Wallace in New Mexico contributed to his pictorial description of the crosscurrents of Jerusalem during the Roman Empire: "*Ben-Hur*, play and novel, may therefore be, unintentionally, a further representation of America—as well as of the New Mexican territory—as a land where disparate cultures rub shoulder; it is a new Holy Land where the solution to harmony is not contention and rebellion (another civil war), but tolerance, democracy, or Christianity."[3]

Ben-Hur: A Tale of the Christ

Wallace's *Ben Hur: A Tale of the Christ*, published by Harper & Brothers, stands as the first significant and most influential novel to deal with the life and times of Jesus Christ. Among those that followed, two stand out. Henryk Sienkiewicz's *Quo Vadis: A Narrative of the Time of Nero* was published in installments in 1895 and appeared as a complete novel in the following year. Known for his historic novels set in his native Poland, Sienkiewicz achieved international acclaim for *Quo Vadis*, which helped the author win the Nobel Prize in Literature in 1905 for his "outstanding merits as an epic writer." The novel has some obvious parallels with *Ben-Hur*, including the two-part title and the subject of a romance set against important historical and religious events. Over sixty years after the initial appearance of *Ben-Hur*, Lloyd

C. Douglas published another seminal novel about Christ, *The Robe* (1942). The author admits to a significant influence from Wallace, but there are even more striking similarities to *Quo Vadis*; both feature a Roman officer named Marcellus led to Christianity by the love of a woman, both show the Roman emperor as insane, and both describe Christians being fed to the lions.

The popular success of *Ben-Hur*, *Quo Vadis*, and *The Robe* can be attributed to their historical accuracy, heroic action, central romantic relationship, and religious underpinnings. Wallace immersed himself in research about the era and worked extensively in the Library of Congress. One example of his historical attention is a detail not shown in the movies. For the march to Calvary, Wallace describes Christ and the other prisoners as carrying only crossbeams, whereas visual recreations invariably show Christ burdened with the entire cross for the obvious symbolism. Wallace also refers to several ancient musical instruments, including the timbrel (ancestor of the tambourine), nebel (lyre), and litui (a shrill type of trumpet). In his research, Wallace read the works of Josephus, a Jewish historian who also bears some striking similarities to the character of Ben-Hur. Josephus fought against the Romans in the First Jewish Roman War (66-73), and, after his capture, eventually attained Roman citizenship.

As for romance and religion, the approach of Wallace differs in emphasis from that of Sienkiewicz and Douglas. Wallace's protagonist is torn between loving two women, Iras (the beautiful Egyptian daughter of Balthasar) and Esther. In the novel, Iras is not as malevolent as in *Ben-Hur: A Tale of the Christ* (1925), and Esther is not the romantic focus as in *Ben-Hur* (1959). But the essence of the protagonist's choice between two females, a seducer and redeemer, is present. In addition, Ben-Hur discovers and follows Christ of his own accord; Wallace allows the male figure to embrace Christianity without female guidance. This contrasts with *Quo Vadis* and *The Robe*, where the woman leads the protagonist to Christianity. This linking of Christianity and femininity is adapted into William Wyler's version of *Ben-Hur*.

Wallace's novel takes on a format common in historical novels with its divisions into a number of large parts or Books, each containing multiple chapters. A similar structure can be found in *The Hunchback of Notre Dame*, *A Tale of Two Cities*, *War and Peace*, and the *Bible* itself. *Ben-Hur* is divided into eight parts (Table 3.1). Of particular note is the placement of the most exciting event of the novel—the chariot race—just after the midpoint of the novel. This is earlier than will be found in the later versions of the story, and allows greater attention to be given to the story of Christ. In order to generate some action during the last third of the novel, Wallace has Messala send two assassins to murder Ben-Hur and has a sword fight between Ben-Hur and a Roman soldier, both of which are omitted in the later versions.

Table 3.1. Structure of the Novel

Section	Plot
Part I	Birth of Christ; Adoration of the Magi
Part II	Twenty-one years later, Ben-Hur and Messala quarrel; following an accident, Ben-Hur is sent to the galleys; Ben-Hur encounters Christ
Part III	Ben-Hur is a galley slave; battle; rescue of Quintus Arrius; Ben-Hur adopted
Part IV	Ben-Hur goes to Antioch; prepares for chariot race against Messala
Part V	Chariot race and aftermath
Part VI	Miriam and Tirzah have leprosy
Part VII	Ben-Hur trains his army; John the Baptist baptizes Christ
Part VIII	Ben-Hur follows Christ; Miriam and Tirzah cured; Crucifixion; Messala murdered; Ben-Hur and Esther have children; Ben-Hur builds San Calixto

Critical and Popular Reception

Critics and the public did not see eye-to-eye on Wallace's novel. The early reviews ranged from cool to hostile, but readers soon discovered the work in mass. Although the initial sales were slow, they picked up rapidly around mid-decade. By the end of the decade, 400,000 copies had been sold; it was the most requested book at public libraries and considered a classic in public schools. Sales continued to grow in the early twentieth century. One million copies were sold by 1912, and *Ben Hur: A Tale of the Christ* set a record in the following year when Sears Roebuck ordered another million copies, the largest order for a novel ever made up to that time. Wallace's book received public endorsements from Presidents Grant, Garfield, and Hayes. Pope Leo XIII gave a special Italian version his blessing, the first ever conferred on a novel by a Pontiff.

A national craze developed for the hero of the story. Several American towns were named Ben Hur, and communities in Virginia, Texas, and California are still known by that name today. A national fraternal organization called the "Supreme Tribe of Ben-Hur" was established in 1893. Its goals were social, humanitarian, and financial—it sold life insurance. The organization maintained close ties to the novel, and membership increased substantially after the 1925 silent film.[4]

Such widespread popularity only fueled the flames for some critics. Hammond Lamont, writing for *The Nation*, called readers of *Ben-Hur* "Philistines" and described them as people who could spend "hours happily and unconsciously while waiting for the gallows."[5] Later twentieth-century assessments are mixed, but few can deny the novel's impact: "Besides *Uncle Tom's Cabin*, among American novels only Owen Wister's *The Virginian* (1902), because it furthered the establishment of the western genre, can be said to have exerted so much influence on middlebrow and popular culture as did *Ben-Hur*."[6] Hanson also ascribes a lofty position for the novel:

> Even as the Boston Brahmins of the literary elite—James Russell Lowell, Oliver Wendell Holmes, Thomas Bailey Aldrich, and William Dean Howells—snubbed Wallace and scoffed at the amateur's clumsy efforts at fiction, the American public bought the book in droves. For many, it became the first—and only—novel they ever read. Whether Wallace realized it or not, godly and self-made Americans identified with Ben-Hur's singular quest for revenge and redemption. Hundreds more readers wrote to Wallace that the novel had in fact convinced them to convert to Christianity. In that regard, *Ben-Hur* marked a radical change in American letters, as millions of Americans for the first time felt that reading fiction was neither sacrilegious nor the sole esoteric pursuit of intellectuals, but was rightly intended for the secular enjoyment and edification of common people. Lew Wallace, as it turned out, introduced more Americans to reading than any other author of the nineteenth century. He, in essence, had invented popular American fiction.[7]

Early Theatrical Interpretations

Popular novels frequently served as material for theatrical renditions during the nineteenth century. Live reenactments ranged from simple dramatic readings to elaborate presentations involving multiple actors or visual images. Many literary stories were ultimately brought to the stage. With the turn of the century, the fledging film industry also turned to popular novels as sources for narratives. During the first four decades after the novel's publication, the story of *Ben-Hur* would be read in churches and private homes, presented in multiple Broadway theaters, and viewed in movie theaters.

Dramatic Readings, Tableaus, and Lantern Shows

Interests in dramatizing *Ben-Hur* are evident as early as 1882. Wallace initially refused requests for readings, tableaus, and even simple songs based on his novel, but that did not always deter intrepid thespians. Mrs. Ellen Knight Bradford, for example, sponsored private performances with seventeen actors and twenty-one tableaus. Among other interpretations, one used 145 richly colored lantern slides. Wallace ultimately had to go to court in order to stop performances by Billy Cleveland and his 'Polite Minstrels' and preserve the dignity of his story. The 1899 production of the author-approved Broadway play did not halt rogue adaptations. In 1912, Mrs. Gurley-Kane raised money for *Titanic* victims in Washington, D.C., with a one-woman presentation; she played eighteen different characters. Her show also included songs from church choirs and music from the U.S. Marine Band.

In the late 1880s and early 1890s, Wallace undertook numerous book tours and gave dramatic readings that were highly successful. In 1891, he created an official libretto for a more sophisticated presentation: *Ben-Hur, in Tableaux and Pantomime*. In keeping with Wallace's convictions, there is no acting part for Christ in this self-proclaimed "spectacular pantomime." His "tale" is primarily inferred from the narration and the miraculous cure of the lepers. Notably, several scenes are devoted to decidedly secular matters, such as the "revelry of the Priestess of Apollo" and the "Arabian girls' frolic." The final scene takes place in Ben-Hur's home in Misenum, where the novel concludes. The audience was then asked to remain seated for a "grand closing allegory" entitled "Iris' Dream of the Nile." A solo pianist provided musical support for these performances.

Broadway Play

Wallace doubted that his book could be brought to the stage, largely because of the complications of the chariot race and the potential difficulties of representing Christ. Marc Klaw and Abraham Erlanger convinced him that these problems could be solved. The chariot race was to be run by two chariots, each with four horses, on treadmills. The background would be a cyclorama that enhanced the visual effect of a race. In addition, the Crucifixion scene would be omitted, and Christ would not be portrayed by an actor, but suggested by a strong beam of light. With these concessions, Wallace assisted William Young in the creation of the script in which much of the original dialogue was retained. Wallace was a constant visitor during rehearsals and naturally attended the premier, along with Florenz Ziegfeld, David Belasco, and dignitaries from his home state of Indiana that included fifty members of the Supreme Tribe of Ben-Hur.

The play, which ran for three and a half hours, consists of a prelude and six acts that roughly conform to the divisions in Wallace's novel (Table 3.2). The material prior to the chariot race is somewhat expanded, and the material that follows is reduced, moving the race closer to the end of the story than it is in the novel. The play concludes with the healing of leprosy at the Mount of Olives and does not deal with the death of Christ or Ben-Hur's later life.

Table 3.2. Structures of the Novel and the Play

Novel	Play	Story
Book I	Prelude	Birth of Christ
Book II	Act I	Accident; Arrest
Book III	Act II	Galley slave; battle; rescue
Book IV	Acts III and IV	Return to Judea; Grove of Daphne; Sheik Ilderim
Book V	Act V	Chariot race
Book VI	Act VI	Leprosy
Book VII	Omitted	Ben-Hur's army; John the Baptist
Book VIII	Act VI	Mount of Olives; Leprosy healed
Book VIII	Omitted	Crucifixion
Epilogue	Omitted	Ben-Hur to build San Calixto

Enhancing the spectacle were live camels, beautiful scenic backdrops, and music. Klaw and Erlanger wanted substantial incidental music and initially asked Edward MacDowell, the composer of the popular "To a Wild Rose" and one of the few American musicians with an international reputation. MacDowell declined and recommended Edgar Stillman Kelley.

Kelley was a well-traveled and versatile musician. He studied music in Germany, worked as an organist and a critic for the *Examiner* in San Francisco, conducted an operetta company in New York, served as a one-year sabbatical replacement for Horatio Parker at Yale, and ended his career in Ohio, teaching at Western College and the Cincinnati Conservatory of Music. He is the author of *Chopin, the Composer* (1913), which is impressive in its historical information, analysis, and critical evaluation. He also wrote *The History of Musical Instruments* (1925), and his knowledge of instruments is apparent in a number of his compositions. Although his musical style is essentially romantic, he did employ late-romantic harmonies and non-Western musical sounds; one work combines oboes, muted trumpets, and mandolins to produce the timbres of Chinese instruments. His *New England Symphony* shows the influence of the Indianist movement with its incorporation of American Indian melodies. It also contains themes based on bird songs.

Kelley's most popular work would become the incidental music for *Ben-Hur*, which mostly consists of preludes, transitions, and choruses.[8] There are several passages of melodrama, and the most popular excerpt is a solo song given to Iras when she enchants Ben-Hur on a boat in the moonlight. The text for the song is from Wallace's novel. There are several recurring musical themes, as observed by Katherine Preston, but their treatment is hardly Wagnerian.[9] The Morsbergers also refer to a leitmotif for Christ, but the only "appearance" of the adult Christ is in the final scene, and this moment has new musical material.[10]

Kelley evokes appropriate moods and styles for various ethnic groups. Preston suggests that this is part of the tradition of toga plays: "Christians in toga plays appear, move, pray, are tortured, encounter the presence of Jesus, are cured of leprosy, and die to music evocative of hymns or other religious compositions. Romans, on the other hand, make love, gamble, race chariots, plot evil deeds, and go to war to music of a frivolous, licentious, or martial character."[11]

Kelley also creates a distinct Middle-Eastern character. For the approaching Magi, he composed an orchestral passage marked "andante misterioso." A marchlike pulse is established in the muted strings with alternating nonresolving seventh chords, and the bassoon and bass clarinet play a flowing, ornamental melody.[12] In addition to standard Roman brass fanfares and a stirring march, Kelley mimics an antique musical style with modal melodies and prominent augmented seconds. In one passage, Kelley accompanies an oboe solo with a mandolin. His harmonic treatment involves cross relations, major and minor alternations, and dissonant tone clusters. The evident craftsmanship supports Rózsa's view on the models for early film music: "It [film music] is derived from incidental theater music, a form which was used largely in the last century."[13]

There are two musical highlights in the 1899 production. The first is in Act III at the Grove of Daphne. Extensive choral singing (the chorus is said to have had 260 members), dancing, and pantomimes celebrate Daphne and Eros. As will be found in the traditions of biblical films, a touch of eroticism seems to be a standard feature for religious dramas. At one point, a young couple is urged to join in love. According to the script: "the maiden again shows coyness, but joins with the youth at last in the wild abandon of the dance which follows." Soon a Devadasi[14] comes forward dancing to a drinking song. Showing his knowledge of ancient instruments, Kelley requested an onstage aulos, an instrument that is associated with Bacchanalian feasts in antiquity. The timbre of the aulos, as in later film scores, is assigned to the orchestral oboe.

The other musical highlight of the play is the finale, Christ at the Mount of Olives. The scene opens with an eight-voice a cappella chorus singing Hosannas. Later, the people of Jerusalem ask who is coming, and the children choir responds with "Jesus Christ of Nazareth," leading to a full choral and orchestral climax. The scene includes a choral rendition of the *Nunc Dimittis*, a canticle from the second chapter of Luke.

With spectacles such as the chariot race (the number of horses eventually increased to twenty with five chariots), a drifting raft, and a ship galley with three tiers of oarsmen, the play became "one of the most phenomenal hits in the history of the American theater."[15] Robert and Katharine Morsberger add:

> Just as the novel broke the fundamentalist prohibition against reading fiction, so the play pacified the puritans and introduced them to the stage, as the 1925 film was to do for the movies. In its wake, other novels with Biblical settings were staged, such as *Quo Vadis* (1901) and *Judith of Bethulia* (1904).... William Jennings Bryan called it 'the greatest play on the stage when measured by its religious tone and moral effect,' and Billy Sunday, the ball player turned evangelist, said, "I wish 100,000,000 people could see the play."[16]

The play closed the 1899 season for the Broadway Theater and opened the 1900 season. Thereafter it was revived on Broadway at various theaters in 1903, 1907, 1911, and 1916. In addition, it traveled around the country and abroad, where it enjoyed record-breaking successes in both London and Australia. Among the dignitaries at the Drury Gardens London premier were Edward VII, Queen Alexandra, Sir Henry Irving, and Sir Arthur Conan Doyle. In all, it is estimated that the play was produced over 6,000 times for a total audience of twenty million people. Victor David Hanson surmises: "In short, the play was the most successful in American history, and to this day has drawn a greater aggregate audience than any dramatic presentation of an American author."[17]

Once again, critical reception did not always match the enthusiasm of the general public. While praising the spectacle of the production, criticisms of actors (including the original Messala played by William S. Hart, who would become one of the most popular stars in Westerns during the silent era) and of the dramatic content were not infrequent. The attitude expressed in the *New York Times* after the premier is typical:

> But there are a few mature playgoers to whom mechanical devices of this sort no longer appeal. So far from being dramatic, such stage pictures are essentially the reverse. They destroy the very illusion they are intended to create in the minds of the sincere dramatic student. Horses galloping from nowhere to nowhere on sliding platforms in front of a quickly rolling panorama; painted canvas shaken from beneath, do not satisfy the imagination that receives the greatest enjoyment from the actor's art. But the multitude is always best pleased with toys.[18]

The music is mentioned several times in reviews, and it is usually described as somewhere between effective and adequate. The reviewer for the *Boston Transcript* was more enthusiastic: "it is so seldom that you hear incidental music that really adds anything to a play; this does. Some strokes are simply capital."[19]

The significance of this play to film history goes beyond its position as a forerunner to the *Ben-Hur* films. The grand nature of the production would serve as a direct model for early epic films, and the financial success of the play did not go unnoticed by D.W. Griffith or Cecil B. DeMille. Within the play we can see standard features adopted by film: a large cast, spectacular sets, extended length, mixture of romance, action, and history, contrasting religious and provocative dance scenes, and a large role for music. Film would incorporate all of these qualities into even bigger presentations (chapter 4).

Early Silent Film

The Kalem Company was founded in 1907 and was sold to Vitagraph in 1917. Despite its relatively short life span, the company distinguished itself with innovative productions. Especially noteworthy was their creation of original piano scores for many of their films.[20] Unfortunately, *Ben Hur*, made in their first year, would not be considered a high point.[21] Director Sidney Olcott borrowed costumes from the Metropolitan opera and created some simple sets. With only a dozen scenes, much of the story had to be omitted. Unless one has prior knowledge of the book or play, the plot makes little sense. The film concludes with the chariot race. In order to save time and money, Olcott filmed a race of firemen who were preparing for a fireworks show. The stationary camera focuses on the excited gesticulations of about a dozen extras, while chariots pass in front periodically. The total effect enraged a young viewer, future director King Vidor:

> I became critical of the scenario, the photography, the acting, the directing. In one scene as Ben-Hur stood on the roof of his home, watching the emperor's chariot, he leaned carelessly against the cornice and freed a loose tile. The chariot was way out in middle of the street and the tile's trajectory was not even near him, yet it fell and struck the emperor. This incongruity so incensed me that I condemned the entire picture.[22]

In addition to its artistic deficiencies, the film was made without prior approval. Klaw and Erlanger, Harper & Brothers, and the Wallace family filed a suit, and the case eventually went to the Supreme Court. In 1911, Chief Justice Oliver Wendell Holmes upheld the rights of the author and his heirs. Since it had already been established that live pantomime violates a copyright, he held that a motion picture pantomime was also an infringement. As a result, Kalem had to withdraw the film from circulation and pay the family $25,000, making their *Ben Hur* the most expensive one-reel film of its time. This ruling would have a major impact on the future of the film industry.

Ben-Hur: A Tale of the Christ (1925)

Once Klaw and Erlanger had successfully blocked Kalem from showing a film version of *Ben-Hur*, the theatrical company turned its attention to making its own silent film based on the play. After lengthy negotiations, a corporation headed by Erlanger, Charles Dillingham, and Florenz Ziegfeld obtained the rights. Several filmmakers vied for the contract to produce *Ben-Hur*, including D.W. Griffith. Ultimately, an agreement was signed with the nascent Metro-Goldwyn-Mayer Inc. for a royalty of fifty percent of the gross receipts. Because of this hefty contract, the lengthy production that involved changes of directors (settling on Frank Niblo), cast, and location (Italy to Hollywood), and the epic sets and numbers of extras, *Ben-Hur: A Tale of the Christ* (1925) became the most expensive film made up to that time. Although it would gross over nine million dollars in its first two years, MGM lost money on the venture. Still the film's quality and popularity established MGM's reputation as Hollywood's foremost studio.

Adaptation

In many respects, the MGM silent film follows the original novel more closely than any other representation. It devotes significant time to the "Tale of the Christ," and the end of the film includes the Crucifixion omitted in the stage play, complete with soldiers gambling for Christ's robe and a spectacular earthquake. In a brief epilogue, Ben-Hur reminds us that Christ lives in our hearts. The film also assimilates a number of the play's interpretations and nuances, the most significant of which is the portrayal of Christ. The background image during the Overture shows a bright light shining down from heaven, a clear reference to Christ's depiction through illumination in the play. Once the narrative begins, the face of the actor portraying Christ is never shown. The presence of Christ is indicated primarily with views of his hands; at times the audience is also shown his back or his footprints.[23]

Interwoven in the manner of *Intolerance* are several biblical scenes, such as the saving of a woman about to be stoned and a Leonardo da Vinci inspired vision of the Last Supper, both of which are not in the novel. While most of the film is in black and white, Niblo uses color for scenes dealing with Christ or his influence. The major exception to this is Ben-Hur's triumphal march through Rome, where the use of color suggests his God-like reception. The color also happens to highlight the bare-breasted women leading the procession. Niblo too was not above adding a touch of sex to a biblical story.

The film alters some of the characters from their Broadway predecessors. Ben-Hur's heroic masculinity is enhanced by his engagement in the battle against pirates and by his militant response once he learns of a King of Jews—he wants to build an army (both events are in the novel). Judah is also shown as an early convert to Christ, and he becomes the family spokesman for Christianity. Although Esther does not lead Ben-Hur to Christ, she still has an expanded role and assimilates some of the actions originally given to Amrah, such as bringing the Lepers to Christ. In the 1959 film, Ben-Hur will assume this role, as he heroically searches for Tirzah and carries her into Jerusalem. As in the novel, Esther has a rival for Ben-Hur's affection in Balthazar's daughter. Iras is presented as a 1920s vamp, showing none of the nuances of her character in Wallace's conception. She is Messala's lover, spies on Ben-Hur, and nurses Messala after the race. The novel's epilogue in which she admits to murdering Messala and commits suicide is omitted.

Music

William Axt and David Mendoza created an original score for *Ben-Hur: A Tale of the Christ*. Among the leading American film composers of the 1920s, the two collaborated on films such as *Greed* (1924), *The Big Parade* (1925), and *Don Juan* (1926), the first full-length feature with synchronized sound. Axt and Mendoza worked for Capitol Theater, one of the major movie palaces in New York. Loew's Theaters acquired the Capitol in 1924, the same year that its founder Marcus Loew gained control of Metro Pictures, Goldwyn Pictures Corporation, and Louis B. Mayer Pictures, thereby forming the MGM studio. From that point, the relationship between Capitol Theater and MGM would be close. MGM would acquire the Capitol Theater music library, which numbered over thirty thousand scores, and the studio sent their major films to New York for scoring. Axt eventually moved to Hollywood and became the head of the music department at MGM. He composed the majority of their early sound scores, including those for *Dinner at Eight* (1933), *Manhattan Melodrama* (1934), and *The Thin Man* (1934).

   Continuing the tradition established by the play, music played a role in the success of *Ben-Hur: A Tale of the Christ*. Blending borrowed and new material, Axt and Mendoza fashioned distinct styles to depict cultural groups: Romans are given fanfares, one of which becomes a leitmotif for Quintus Arrius and for Rome in general; Arabian music is suggested with modal scales and mild dissonances for the Wise Men, a lively ethnic dance for Sheik Ilderim, and a seductive chromatic theme for Iras; and the mention of Judea or the current state of Jewish people invariably brings out a C-minor chord followed by a variety of solemn dissonances.

   In general, leitmotifs are used sparingly, much less than in the Axt and Mendoza score to *Don Juan*. The recurring themes generally retain their original pitch center. Christ has a simple theme consisting of four pitches that are within a pentatonic scale (Example 3.1). In keeping with the tradition of reflecting the Trinity in the music, Christ's key is

E-flat (three flats), and the theme begins with the ascent of a third and generally remains within that range.

Example 3.1. *Ben-Hur: A Tale of the Christ*, Christ Theme.

Ben-Hur has two themes: one for his heroic nature and one for his love of Esther. The former is somewhat understated, but the latter is lyric, harmonically rich, and presented warmly in the strings. Throughout, the score is colorful, the harmonies varied, and the moods effective. A shorter version of the film was released in 1931 with the recorded music of Axt and Mendoza, but this is not currently available for viewing.

Ben-Hur (1959)

Facing a financial crisis in the 1950s, MGM turned once again to *Ben-Hur*. Recalling the triumph of the silent film and bolstered by the success of *Quo Vadis*, the studio hired director William Wyler and spent five years preparing for the blockbuster. Massive sets were created, scenes were shot on location in Italy, an enormous cast was gathered that included 10,000 extras with 365 speaking roles, 100,000 costumes were made, and the resultant picture extended 212 minutes, the longest Hollywood feature film made in the sound era other than *Gone With the Wind* (238 minutes) and *The Ten Commandments* (220 minutes). The film grossed nearly $40 million in its first year, thereby becoming the studio's largest moneymaker after *Gone With the Wind*. Unfortunately, the financial reprieve was only temporary. Attempts to recapture the success of *Ben-Hur* with films such as *Cimarron* (1960), *King of Kings* (1961), and *Mutiny on the Bounty* (1962) contributed to the studio's continued decline.

Adaptation

Karl Tunberg created the screenplay for the film with contributions from Maxwell Anderson, Samuel Nathaniel Behrman, Christopher Fry, and Gore Vidal. Despite its length, the narrative for Wyler's *Ben-Hur* is simpler in many respects than those for the earlier versions. Some of the liberties taken with the story weaken the overall dramatic thrust, but for the most part they enhance the film's public appeal and create a clearer structure (See Table 3.3).

Table 3.3. Structure of *Ben-Hur* (1959)

Section	Plot
Christ Exposition	Jerusalem; Joseph and Mary
	The North Star and the Wise Men
	The Nativity
Ben-Hur Exposition	Messala returns to Jerusalem
	Ben-Hur and Messala renew friendship
Judea	Ben-Hur and Messala become enemies
	Ben-Hur and Esther fall in love
	The roof tile injures Gratus
	Ben-Hur and family are arrested
Exile	Desert march
	Christ offers water
	Galley slave
	Sea battle
	Ben-Hur saves Quintus Arrius
	Ben-Hur goes to Rome as a hero
	Arrius adopts Ben-Hur
Judea	Ben-Hur returns to Judea
	Meets Sheik Ilderim and Balthazar
	Ben-Hur reunites with Esther
	Miriam and Tirzah are lepers
	Ben-Hur wins chariot race
	Messala dies; tells Ben-Hur about family
	Ben-Hur seeks family
	Ben-Hur takes Miriam and Tirzah to see Christ
	Christ carries cross; Ben-Hur offers water
Climax and Resolution	Christ is crucified
	Storm spreads Christ's blood throughout land
	Miriam and Tirzah are cured of leprosy
	Ben-Hur finds peace
	Ben-Hur reunites with Esther and family
	The Resurrection is implied

Since there are two principal stories in the narrative, the film provides two expositions—one for Christ and one for Ben-Hur. Both are given musical preludes. The series of complications is derived from Ben-Hur's life. These can be divided into three parts: Judea, Exile, and Judea. The Crucifixion initiates a rapid climax and resolution for both stories.

With these alterations to the original story, the plot takes on a mirror-like structure in which the outer frames show the birth and the death of Christ. The turning point in the drama takes place during the sea battle. Left unchained, Ben-Hur leaves the lower deck and climbs to the upper deck, symbolically moving from slavery to freedom. He soon rescues Quintus Arrius and pulls him onto a makeshift raft, where he is now the commander and Arrius is in chains. Esther's expanded role contributes to this structure; for the first time, she has a strong presence in the first half of the story, and she and Judah talk of love in the upstairs chamber. This scene is repeated in the same room during the second half, but their loving words turn bitter, as Judah has gone from love to hate—in essence, he has, like Messala, returned to Judea as a Roman. In the first half, Messala condemns Ben-Hur to death, and in the second, Ben-Hur causes the death of Messala. Perhaps the most dramatic reversal is seen in the two moments when Ben-Hur and Christ have contact. During Ben-Hur's death march through the desert, Jesus offers him water, which rejuvenates his spirit. Later in the film, Ben-Hur recognizes Jesus during his death march and offers him water. In both instances, a Roman guard intervenes, but with contrasting results. These parallel death marches have precedents in the silent film, but do not occur in the novel.

Ben-Hur's character is given greater masculine strength and a higher level of vulnerability in the film. His strength is built through the trials of fire (the burning desert march), water (surviving a shipwreck), and wind (the chariot race), but his victories have no value without his family, the source of his vulnerability. These two sides of his character are established early in the film. The accident with the roof tile is shown to be the fault of Tirzah, not Ben-Hur. With this change, the film retains Judah's image of athleticism (not prone to clumsy accidents) and projects his protectiveness of the family when he takes the blame. These qualities come into further prominence in the following scene, which was newly created for the film. Ben-Hur is shown in the prison at the Antonio Fortress. With physical bravura, he escapes from the guards and confronts Messala. Holding a threatening javelin in hand, Ben-Hur can have quick revenge. But Messala exploits his vulnerability—his concern and love for his mother and sister; Judah throws the spear into the wall and is taken to be a galley slave.

The driving force of the film is the relationship between the two former best friends. In the novel, Ben-Hur is a boy of about seventeen and not a match for the more mature Messala. In this film version, Ben-Hur is already seen as physically equal if not superior to Messala. Indeed, Messala seems to need devious means to gain the upper hand, such as threatening Judah's family or having spikes on the wheels of his chariot (these are not present in any previous rendition). Messala is shown for the most part to be detached and self-serving. Only a couple of brief moments reveal his past emotional attachment to Judah. In the silent film, anti-Semitism is much more pronounced amongst the Romans, and Messala is embarrassed by his former friendship with a Jew. In the sound film, Messala is excited to be reunited with his childhood friend and chastises the guard announcing Ben-Hur's presence for not treating him with dignity. The other telling moment is also an addition to the 1959 film. After the arrest, Messala stands on the rooftop where he and young Judah used to play. He discovers that the tiles are indeed loose and that the incident was simply an accident, but he remains silent. Rózsa's ironic playing of the Friendship theme in a warm string timbre underscores Messala's sacrificing of his personal feelings for political gain.

A mild controversy has developed over Gore Vidal's suggestion that the script intended to imply a youthful homosexual relationship between Ben-Hur and Messala. According to Vidal, Messala's actions were to be seen as those of a rejected lover.[24] Today, one can read into the dialogue and actions (throwing spears into the crossbeam) some suggestions of this interpretation, but most theatergoers of the late 1950s and early 1960s would have been oblivious to any such implications, and an overt presence of this subplot would have undermined the masculinity of the protagonist. There is a suggestion though that Messala has returned to Jerusalem with a male relationship, his constant companion Drusus. Particularly suggestive is the scene in which we see Drusus in the feminine role of reading while Messala is engaging in the masculine activity of practicing his whip.

Ben-Hur's strength of character is also enhanced with the absence of Iras, a major character in the novel, play, and silent film. No longer does Judah come under the spell of a seductress, nor does Balthasar have a daughter of questionable morality. As a result, Messala dies after the race rather than from the hands of his Egyptian lover. Iras was originally included in the script and given the cliché of a bath scene.

Her eventual elimination, along with the entire scene at the Grove of Daphne, removes the primary erotic elements from the plot. Like *The Ten Commandments* from three years earlier, the 1959 *Ben-Hur* is more wholesome than any of the earlier versions.

Esther's role also benefits from the lack of female competition. Esther can now be introduced near the beginning of the story, much earlier than in the novel. She and Ben-Hur fall in love prior to the roof incident, and Judah retains his love for her throughout his trials (in spite of that woman companion hanging on his arm at the Roman feast). Esther remains pure and faithful during this time, as she embodies the essence of Christian love. Conforming to the ideal of a woman leading a man to Christianity established in silent film epics, this version of the Wallace story shows Judah as resistant to the teachings of Christ; Ben-Hur's Christian activities in the novel, such as leading an army and devoting his fortune to a new religion, are omitted altogether. Judah's evident conversion, the Crucifixion, the spreading of Christ's blood throughout the land, the healing of leprosy, and the reuniting of a family are all condensed into a brief span that serves as a potent emotional climax for Wyler's epic.

Reception

Critics, although not unanimous, tended to agree with the audiences' enthusiasm.[25] A review in *Variety* typifies the critical response: "The big difference between *Ben-Hur* and other spectacles, biblical or otherwise, is the sincere concern for human beings. They're not just pawns reciting flowery dialog to fill gaps between the action and spectacle scenes. They arouse genuine emotional feeling in the audience."[26] The Academy honored *Ben-Hur* with twelve nominations and eleven wins, including Best Actor, Best Director, Best Picture, and Best Music. The number of Oscars was the most ever given to a film up to that point, and only *Titanic* and *The Lord of the Rings: The Return of the King* have matched the record since. Among the competing films in 1959 were the classics *Anatomy of a Murder*, *Room at the Top*, and *Some Like It Hot*. Another major film from that year was François Truffaut's *Les quatre cents coups* (*The 400 Blows*). Truffaut helped spark the French New Wave, whose products can be seen as the antithesis of Hollywood epics. Yet, he admired *Ben-Hur*, noting that the picture combined "commerciality and experimentality" in the manner of Hitchcock's films.[27]

Rózsa's score contributed greatly to the success of the film. Most of the initial reviews focused on the drama and spectacle, giving Rózsa brief acknowledgment. But the music soon developed a life of its own. For the first time, two LPs were released for an original film score. The first, issued in 1960, received a Grammy nomination and spent 98 weeks on the *Billboard* charts, where it rose as high as number six.

Individual musical excerpts from the film also achieved a high level of popularity. *The Parade of the Charioteers* became common material for wind ensembles, particularly for the emerging American marching band, while the "Love Theme" was arranged for school string ensembles. The "Adoration of the Magi" (SSA), "Mother's Love" (SATB), "Star of Bethlehem" (SATB), and the closing music, "*The Christ Theme (Alleluia)*" (SATB and TTBB) were sung in churches and schools, and the opening *Ben-Hur* Overture was performed in symphonic concert halls. Sales of piano excerpts were also extremely profitable. Few film scores prior to *Star Wars* enjoyed as much popular success and had as much influence as Rózsa's music for *Ben-Hur*.[28] In his autobiography, Rózsa writes of his personal attachment to the music: "I won my third Oscar for that score, and it is the one I cherish the most. The music of *Ben-Hur* is close to my heart."[29]

Into the Twenty-First Century

Ben-Hur would conquer yet one more medium—television. Broken into four installments, Wyler's film made its primetime debut in 1971 and received the highest rating of any movie presented on television up to that time. Although not on such a grand scale, Wallace's story has survived into the twenty-first century. Several musical versions have appeared, and a Canadian television series began in 2010 with Joseph Morgan cast as Ben-Hur.

In 2003, an animated *Ben Hur* was released on video. Elements of the Wyler film are apparent in this animation, but it draws upon details from the novel as well. Proportionally, it devotes substantially more time to the story of Christ. A synthesized musical score provided by Keith Heffner and Michael Lloyd mimics a symphonic orchestra, choir, and an occasional rock beat and provides suitable cues suggesting Roman, Jewish, Christian, and Arabic worlds. This modest animated production features the voice of Charlton Heston as Ben Hur, his last acting role before passing in 2008.

Twenty-first-century criticism of the 1959 film has retained the conflicting views that have followed the *Ben-Hur* story since the nineteenth century. This contradiction can even be seen in the implied values of the American Film Institute and their selections of the nation's best movies (Table 3.4). In its 2008 list of America's top ten epic films, *Ben-Hur* is second, behind *Lawrence of Arabia* and just ahead of *Schindler's List* and *Gone With the Wind*. But in the 2007 list of America's top 100 movies, *Ben-Hur* is dead last at 100, well behind *Gone With the Wind*, *Lawrence of Arabia*, and *Schindler's List*, as well as three other "epics" that were below *Ben-Hur* on the 2008 list: *Saving Private Ryan*, *Spartacus*, and *Titanic*.

Table 3.4. Comparison of AFI Rankings

Film	Top Epics	Top 100 Films
Lawrence of Arabia	1	7
Ben-Hur	2	100
Schindler's List	3	8
Gone With the Wind	4	6
Spartacus	5	81
Titanic	6	83
All Quiet on the Western Front	7	unlisted
Saving Private Ryan	8	71
Reds	9	unlisted
The Ten Commandments	10	unlisted

These observations are not meant to belittle the entertaining AFI film lists, as they provide a useful forum to spark debates about films. But this contradiction reveals lingering and unwarranted modernist biases against popular monumental films: *Ben-Hur* is great when considered as an epic, but the assessment of its quality diminishes when measured against films from other genres. The attitude is unfortunate. *Ben-Hur* is one of Hollywood's greatest successes. Even discarding the facts that it was the highest box-office winner of a decade and the winner of eleven Oscars, it is an outstanding artistic achievement with a brilliant screenplay, dynamic acting, award-winning cinematography, and monumental music. It also represents the culminating point of biblical epic films, as will be discussed in chapter 4.

4

THE MUSIC AND ITS CONTEXT

Rózsa's music for *Ben-Hur* seems decidedly conservative in light of the changes that were taking place in Hollywood film scoring during the 1950s. There could be no stronger contrast between current and past trends than with the scores of *Anatomy of a Murder* (Duke Ellington) and *Ben-Hur*, rivals for the Best Picture award in 1959. Even within the conventions for epic films, *The Bridge on the River Kwai* (1957) had established a new approach to scoring in which the amount of music was limited, and a single popular-styled melody dominated the score. This alternative to wall-to-wall scoring was later assimilated into films such as *Exodus* (1960), *Lawrence of Arabia* (1962), and *Doctor Zhivago* (1965), all of which won Oscars for Best Score.

Yet, *Ben-Hur* is best understood not against the backdrop of these contemporary movies, but within the narrow context of epic films set in antiquity. The Mediterranean region provides the primary location for a variety of cinematic narratives dating back to the Roman Era and before. Nonbiblical stories, which include stories in Egypt, Mesopotamia, Macedonia/Greece, and non-Christian Rome, generally center on large conflicts and spectacular scenes. *Old Testament* reenactments are filled with colorful heroes, while accounts from the *New Testament* tend to be more intimate. Since stories of the life of Christ are limited in romance, conflict, and spectacle, plots inspired by the *New Testament* often interweave fictional stories with the life of Jesus or focus on martyrdom during the early years of Christianity.

Despite these differences, epic movies about ancient times share in common numerous features that were developed during three principal phases: the silent era established the defining qualities of the genre; sound films from the 1930s introduced several distinct characteristics, most notably in the music; and a biblical revival beginning in 1949 resurrected and built upon these traditions. The latter movement culminated with *Ben-Hur*. Since the narrative and score for *Ben-Hur* rely heavily upon generic conventions, an overview of epic films set in antiquity is necessary to understand the mixture of clichés and innovations that contributed to *Ben-Hur's* remarkable success.

Silent Era Epics

Narrative Conventions

Building on models established with theater productions like *Ben-Hur* (see chapter 3), Italian filmmakers created the earliest films with epic proportions. The common characteristics of the new genre include monumental sets, hundreds of extras, and vivid images that could not be duplicated on stage. Among the Italian movies set in ancient times, two are particularly noteworthy: *Quo Vadis?* (1912) and *Cabiria* (1914). With a running time of nearly two hours, *Quo Vadis?* is the first feature-length film in cinema history. Meaning "Where are you going?," *Quo Vadis?* is based on the Henryk Sienkiewicz novel in which two fictional love stories are interwoven with the apocryphal account of Saint Peter's encounter with the spirit of Christ, his return to Nero's Rome, and his head-down crucifixion. In addition to the film's unprecedented length, the movie exhibits epic qualities that include massive sets, 3,000 extras, and spectacles such as Rome burning, a chariot race, and lions feasting on Christians.

Cabiria became the model for future epics. Jon Solomon notes: "Of all the Italian epics of the silent Golden Age, *Cabiria* best demonstrated to subsequent filmmakers how to make a successful, full-length, visually crowded, narratively energetic film sprinkled liberally with bits of historical detail and special effects."[1] Set during the Second Punic War, much of the film was shot on location in the Alps, Sicily, and Tunisia. The sets are often spectacular, highlighted by a towering child-devouring furnace. Historic reenactments include the eruption of Etna, Hannibal crossing the Alps, and the mythical destruction of a Roman fleet by the Archimedes heat ray.

In these two films, several stock characters with parallels to *Ben-Hur* can be observed. Both feature lovers consisting of a heroic Roman soldier (Ben-Hur will become a Roman citizen) and an innocent woman. In *Quo Vadis?*, the Roman general Marcus Vinicius falls in love with Lygia. Their romance, his conversion to Christianity, and their martyrdom create a common cycle in films set in the early Christian-Roman world. In these stories, Christianity is equated with love, and the conversion of a Roman soldier inspired by a woman symbolizes Rome's eventual adoption of the Christian religion. In *Cabiria*, the Roman Fulvius is action oriented and vows to protect Cabiria. His many trials include a desert trek, where he, like Ben-Hur, nearly dies from the lack of water. Cabiria blossoms into a beautiful woman, and her virtue and wholesomeness adumbrate qualities in Christian heroines such as Esther.

Another important figure in both films is the strongman protector, Urso in *Quo Vadis?* and Maciste in *Cabiria*. The latter immediately spawned a number of Maciste movies, and he can be seen as a forerunner to the Herculean characters in later Italian movies. The combination of a faithful servant and a strongman protector has contemporary parallels in an expanded role for Urso in the remake of *Quo Vadis* (1951), and Victor Mature's character in *The Robe* (1953) and *Demetrius and the Gladiators* (1954). In Wyler's *Ben-Hur*, the faithful servant is of course Simonides, but the script turns his servant Malluch into a strongman protector for Esther, a quality that is not in the original novel.

The enormous financial success of *Cabiria* inspired filmmakers in America. D.W. Griffith created two epics that have settings in antiquity, *Judith of Bethulia* (1914) and *Intolerance: Love's Struggle Throughout the Ages* (1916). *Judith of Bethulia*, America's first four-reel movie, is a retelling of the biblical heroine's daring entrance into the camp of the Assyrian Prince Holofernes. She beheads the leader while he sleeps and thereby saves Bethulia from destruction. The story allows for lengthy battle scenes, which includes the use of chariots. *Intolerance* is one of the most influential films of the silent era. Jon Solomon notes: "Had it not been for Griffith's film, there might never have been a *Ben-Hur* or a *Ten Commandments* or any other historic epic after the Italian Golden Age."[2] The film intertwines four stories dealing with love and intolerance, each from a different time period. The most spectacular segment is the re-creation of the conquest of Babylon in 539 B.C., which features siege machines, battles with hundreds of extras, and monumental sets.

One of the other threads in *Intolerance* shows episodes in the life of Jesus. These scenes invariably follow a segment of the "modern" narrative, in which a mother loses her baby due to the prejudices of high society. This linking of Jesus to a fictional story establishes an important model. This pattern more typically involves a second plot set in the time of Christ, as in *Ben-Hur*, but *Intolerance* spawned a series of moralizing films that combined stories in the ancient and contemporary worlds.

Three major Hollywood biblical epics appeared during the 1920s: *The Ten Commandments* (1923), *Ben-Hur: A Tale of the Christ* (1925), and *King of Kings* (1927). Fred Niblo directed *Ben-Hur*, which is discussed in chapter 3. Cecil B. DeMille, who supplanted D.W. Griffith as the leading American director of epics, created the other two. *The Ten Commandments* is the best known of the ancient moralizing films that follows *Intolerance*. The film presents a fifty-minute abbreviated version of Moses in Egypt and at Mt. Sinai (the story begins at a point that is two hours and thirty-five minutes into the 1956 remake) and then segues to a modern story of a young man who refuses to believe in the Commandments. The Moses story allows DeMille to create some stunning scenes, including Jewish slaves building Egyptian monuments and the parting of the Red Sea. *The King of Kings* is a retelling of the story of Christ and includes a spectacular earthquake at the Crucifixion.

Music and Dance Conventions

The stage version of *Ben-Hur* inserts a decidedly secular moment into the otherwise religion-oriented plot. At the Grove of Daphne, dancers and singers celebrate love in an extended scene that includes an onstage replica of an aulos. The entertainment value of an erotic dance number and the effort to suggest authenticity with the image of an antique musical instrument were qualities that were assimilated into the early cinematic epics. *Quo Vadis?* contains several images of music making; Nero sings and plays the kithara while Rome burns, dancers beat on hand drums, and two kithara players perform during the double suicide of Petronius and Eunice. *Cabiria* shows two different musical ensembles in which women play percussion, a panpipe, and various types of harps. The most intriguing looking harp is played between the legs and has a crescent shape with the bottom third expanding like the head of a cobra snake. This peculiar design was likely modeled after an image on a relief of a tomb from the Twelfth Dynast (2000-1800 B.C.).[3] *Cabiria* also features an athletic dance performed by a scantily dressed Nubian female. In the context of this and later films, a barbaric, erotic dance symbolizes a decadent society or ruler.

Images of dancing and musical ensembles are common in American epics as well. *Judith of Bethulia* devotes a substantial amount of time to a bacchanalian dance accompanied by ancient harps and percussion. The Babylonian segments of *Intolerance* contain several dances with authentic-looking musical instruments. DeMille also inserts an erotic dance and all-female orchestra into *King of Kings*.

DeMille's most striking use of dance and music is in *The Ten Commandments*. In this film, three nonbelievers are juxtaposed—the Egyptians, the Jewish revelers, and the modern man and wife. All three are shown with dancing. Exotic dancers entertain the Pharaoh, allowing for a close-up of a musical ensemble consisting of a variety of harps and a flute. Moses observes the dance and disdainfully shakes his head. The orgiastic dancing of the Jewish revelers is a stunning visual highlight, with its hundreds of synchronized dancers and the accompaniment of large drums and other percussion. In the modern story, DeMille provides us with an early film example of the linking of jazz and decadence. When the young couple is dancing to a record on a Sunday, the mother enters and breaks the disc. The audience gets a brief glimpse at the label; "I've Got Those Sunday Blues" performed by The Missourians on a Victor label. The Missourians were a black jazz group that would later merge with Cab Calloway and perform at the Cotton Club. As in many subsequent films in the decade, jazz is portrayed as the portal to sin, decadence, and destruction.

Musical Accompaniment

One of the major contributions of epics to future filmmaking is the attention given to the musical accompaniment; most were presented with original musical scores written for large orchestras. The association of epic films and quality musical support was established at the onset of the genre. Both of the Italian epics discussed above were shown in Italy and in the United States with newly created scores. Rothapfel presented *Quo Vadis?* four times daily in New York, two with organ and two "deluxe" shows with orchestra, choir, and lecturer. A description of the event appeared in *Moving Picture World*:

> After Mr. Calhoun had given a brief story of the film the heavy asbestos curtain was raised to singing and displayed the orchestra garlanded in flowers. The singers' romantic recesses on each side of the stage were also festooned in greenery. Three re-

sounding blasts from trumpets accompanied by the rest of the
orchestra started the entertainment proper on its way.[4]

The adapted score included operatic excerpts drawn from *Faust, Tann-
häuser, Tosca,* and *Parsifal.* According to the reviewer, "the music
alone was well worth the admission price. It is difficult to estimate the
value of such appropriate accompaniment."[5]

American theaters continued to present epics in this manner.
Cabiria was shown in New York with an ensemble featuring over fifty
orchestra members and a chorus. The score, which was created in Italy,
contained excerpts from a number of classical works. Joseph Carl Breil,
who had already provided original music for *Queen Elizabeth* and
would become the most important American film composer in the early
silent film era, claims to have inserted some of his own music. Other
than *Judith of Bethulia,* all of Griffith's epics have newly-created
scores, including Breil's landmark music for *The Birth of a Nation*
(1915). Axt and Mendoza composed music for the silent version of
Ben-Hur (see chapter 3), and Hugo Riesenfeld provided original scores
for both *The Ten Commandments* and *The King of Kings.*

Because of the inherent difficulties in studying music from this
period, the prevalence of ethnic and historical styles in silent film
scores is hard to ascertain. For *Ben-Hur,* Axt and Mendoza made a
modest attempt to create an historical style and to distinguish between
ethnic groups. The Riesenfeld scores, by contrast, reveal little effort
towards developing an ancient style.

Some of the early films with synchronized sound suggest that
composers were aware of musical ethnicity. For *Don Juan* (1926), the
first vitaphone film, William Axt assigns a Sarabande theme to the father figure, which is accurate both regionally and historically. In the
following year, Louis Silvers, writing for *The Jazz Singer,* consistently
provides Russian or Jewish music for scenes inside the house of Cantor
Rabinowitz, an immigrant Russian Jew.

Erno Rapée's *Motion Picture Moods for Pianists and Organists*
(1924), an anthology of musical excerpts for keyboard players accompanying silent films, contains a number of excerpts for identifying national and regional locales. One subtitle contains "Oriental" music,
which includes Arabian music. Most of the excerpts contain clichés
established in the repertory of nineteenth-century orchestral music;
Chinese music is primarily pentatonic, and Arabian music has augmented-second intervals and, at times, parallel chords. There are no
excerpts in the anthology for antiquity or other historical eras. The

creation of more distinctive historical and ethnic styles in cinema would take place in the 1930s.

The Early Sound Era

DeMille Films

With the advent of sound, epic films declined in number and grandeur. Cecil B. DeMille continued to create epic films into the 1930s, but on a smaller scale. He produced two works with plots set in the ancient world, *The Sign of the Cross* (1932) and *Cleopatra* (1934). Rudolph G. Kopp, a prolific film composer during the first half of the decade, supplied music for both. In these scores, he established a number of musical qualities that would become standard in subsequent epics.

The Sign of the Cross derives its title and plot from Wilson Barrett's 1896 stage play. The central figures are once again a Roman military figure and a Christian woman. Also appearing in this film is an easily manipulated, effeminate Nero. He burns Rome while playing a kithara, blames the Christians, and, in the dramatic climax, feeds Christians to the lions. While *The Sign of the Cross* may not have the monumental sets of the silent epics, it did manage to create a sensation with Claudette Colbert's nude scene in a milk bath, a lesbian dance sequence, and some grandly staged arena spectacles, including Amazons fighting Pygmies, elephants crushing humans, alligators converging on a young Christian female, and what might be interpreted as the rape of a nude woman tied to a stake by an ape. As evidenced in earlier films, DeMille is not above adding scintillating sex to a Christian story.

The music for *The Sign of the Cross* is substantial and somewhat sophisticated considering its early date in the sound era. The opening scene mixes source music—Nero playing a kithara—with the scoring for the burning of Rome. Later in the film, a battle of songs develops, as the erotic "The Naked Moon" competes with a Christian chorus; the Christian singers predominate. In several extended cues, ambiguity is created as to whether the music is diegetic or nondiegetic. The second scene of the film cuts to a beggar playing a tibia (aulos). Kopp mimics the sound of the instrument with an oboe and other solo woodwinds. The timbre continues faintly for four and half minutes under several dialogues, during which the cue gradually evolves into scoring. Similar passages can be heard in court with the sound of a harp and flute floating through the rooms. These scenes have a musical parallel in *Ben-*

Hur during the moments when Judah and Esther talk in the upper chamber room.

Kopp's most important contribution to generic conventions of biblical epics in the sound era is the establishment of contrasting aural worlds for Romans and Christians. The Roman world is primarily heard through its source music—fanfares, marches, and decadent party music. Multiple fanfares are played on a bucina, and the games are announced with fanfares from horse-riding cornicines.[6] A Roman march is heard at the intermission and is reprised for the parade of gladiators, but it lacks the forceful qualities of Rózsa's marches. As for the Christians, they are represented with unaccompanied singing, although the melodies are closer to Protestant hymns than chant, especially when they break into four-part harmony.

Kopp similarly creates two musical worlds in *Cleopatra* for the Romans and the Egyptians. Once again the Roman world is heard through its fanfares and marches. Both Julius Caesar and Marc Antony have personalized fanfares, and Caesar's fanfare is the basis for the principal Roman march. Kopp's music for the Egyptian world is significantly richer than that of the Christians in *The Sign of the Cross*. Cleopatra's melody, which suggests a Phyrgian mode, has multiple augmented-second intervals and is first heard with a pair of oboes and a light rhythmic accompaniment that includes harp and bells. In many scenes, the sound of a harp suggests ongoing source music in her palace.

The two musical worlds are juxtaposed and combined on several occasions. For the procession through Rome, Caesar's entrance is preceded by cornicines on horses playing his march. Cleopatra follows with an exotic processional based on her theme that includes quick, repetitive rhythmic patterns in the timpani and jangling shakers. For the climactic confrontation between Roman legions and Egyptian forces led by Marc Antony, Kopp initially mixes Roman fanfares and Egyptian melodic motives in a discordant action cue. Ultimately, fanfares and a march emerge with the Roman victory.

The visual and musical highlight of the film is Cleopatra's seduction of Marc Antony aboard her ship. Numerous exotic dances with appropriate musical accompaniment dazzle the Roman leader. Egyptian musicians can be seen on both sides of the hull with a variety of harps, a wind instrument that is equivalent to the Roman tuba (a long trumpet), and a plucked instrument. When the seduction is complete, Cleopatra's theme gradually turns from its exotic modal qualities to a full romantic orchestral setting in a major key. As the ship sails, the hortator rhythmically hits the drum once every two measures, under-scoring the enormous difference between the warship of Ben-Hur and the love boat of Cleopatra.

Other Films

The only other significant biblical film of the decade is RKO's *The Last Days of Pompeii* (1935). Based on Edward Bulwer-Lytton's novel, the contrived plot manipulates historic time lines in order for Marcus, a blacksmith turned slave hunter for gladiator games, to take his son to Judea, where he encounters Christ and witnesses the Crucifixion. Forty years later, with the boy now just a young man, Marcus redeems himself during the eruption of Mount Vesuvius. Roy Webb's nonstop score does not help the convoluted plot. Musical orientalisms abound, including pentatonic scales and parallel chords, but there is no consistency to their application. Moreover, extended passages from Max Steiner's score for *King Kong* (1933) are borrowed, including the use of the sacrificial dance music to accompany the parade of barbarian horsemen at the games. Webb's most original touch is the use of the vibraphone and high strings for the physical appearances of Christ, an influential combination of timbres that can be found in numerous later Biblical films, including *Ben-Hur*.

Although the number of biblical epics during the decade is limited, important musical qualities for the genre were created in other films. Herbert Stothart and Dimitri Tiomkin established many of the clichés for ethnic settings. For the 1932 historical drama *Rasputin and the Empress*, Stothart takes advantage of Russian source music (Tchaikovsky's *Waltz of the Flowers*), quotes Russian tunes such as "God Save the Tsar" (as does Rózsa in *Knight Without Armour*), and incorporates choral singing in the Russian tradition to suggest the story's locale. More sophisticated renderings of ethnic styles can be seen in the Mexican dance rhythms in *Viva Villa!* (1934) and the pentatonic scales and oriental orchestrations that dominate the score for *The Good Earth* (1937). In the same year, which coincides with Rózsa's first scores for Korda, Dimitri Tiomkin created an extended exotic score complete with parallel harmonies for *The Lost Horizon*.

While examples of ethnic styles are abundant, composers of the 1930s did little to suggest historical styles outside of source music. An exception is Stothart's music for *Romeo and Juliet* (1936), which incorporates a harpsichord, recorders, and excerpts from Peter Warlock's *Capriol Suite*. A few years later, Stothart returns to more traditional colors for *Marie Antoinette* (1938). The film contains a brief harpsichord solo in the overture, an abundance of appropriate diegetic dance music, and an operatic performance of Gluck's *Orpheus et Euridice*. But the music retains the harmonic, melodic, and orchestral qualities of the standard Hollywood practices.

Perhaps the most influential score from the 1930s on films such as *Ben-Hur* is Steiner's *Gone With the Wind*. In this work, Steiner provided a model of how to compose a lengthy score that is both diverse and unified. Over a dozen leitmotifs and other prominent themes are interwoven, allowing each to sound fresh in their appropriate contexts. Nineteenth-century Southern tunes are quoted freely, and ethnic indicators include a ragtime tune for Mammy and an Irish jig for Gerald O'Hara. Rózsa certainly would have noted the effectiveness and popularity of the Tara theme. He assimilated a similar grand sweep in a number of his works, and he must have observed that the tune, other than the expressive appoggiatura in the third measure, is theoretically based on a pentatonic scale.

Revival

Hollywood's postwar difficulties spurred a revival of epic movies set in antiquity. Responding to political attacks and public anxieties over the Cold War, Hollywood produced a series of biblical films that showed positive moral values and the struggle against tyranny. In many of these films, the Soviet Union was symbolically equated with pagan Rome, and the ultimate Christian victory over the empire held a message of hope to American audiences. Cecil B. DeMille's explicit linking of religion and liberty in the prologues to both *Samson and Delilah* and *The Ten Commandments* is critical to the understanding of these films and this era.

With the loss of revenues and the competition of television, filmmakers turned to color, widescreens, and stereo in order to create a unique theatrical experience that could not be duplicated at home. Well suited to the new technology were monumental sets and emotional dramas about religion and freedom. Biblical epics helped pave the way for the Hollywood blockbuster. *Samson and Delilah* (1949) initiated a series of box-office sensations that culminated with *The Ten Commandments* (1956) and *Ben-Hur* (1959). All three of these films are the highest grossing non-Disney films of their respective decades.

Supplying music for these epics were some of Hollywood's finest composers, including Victor Young, Alfred Newman, Franz Waxman, and Miklós Rózsa. Two opposing musical trends emerged. The first, established by Victor Young's *Samson and Delilah*, is a melody-dominated style based in part on musical practices established during the 1930s. The second, initiated by Alfred Newman's *David and Bathsheba* (1951), incorporates techniques of contemporary music in order to create a greater sense of authenticity. Rózsa's music can be seen as a synthesis of these two approaches.

Victor Young

Samson and Delilah was an ideal vehicle for DeMille, as the biblical story featured the popular figures of an ancient strongman and a seductive female. The image of the captured Samson pushing a circular stone grain grinder is a visual parallel to a scene in the silent film *Cabiria*, where Maciste is forced to do the identical task. The building of strength during captivity is a theme that will reappear in *Ben-Hur*.

Also establishing a trend for the next decade, DeMille uses uncharacteristic restraint in treating Delilah and the erotic elements of the story. The climactic bacchanal, for example, is not depicted as an orgy, but as a relatively wholesome family entertainment resembling a circus act. Moreover, Delilah's femme fatale character is softened. The story is altered so that Delilah (Hedy Lamarr) has reasonable motivation for her treachery. Later, she is shown to be remorseful, truly loving of Samson, and willing to die with him in the temple. The music plays a role in this characterization, as her seductive theme turns genuine when she asks to be forgiven and assists the blind Samson. The creation of sympathetic biblical femme fatales is an important thread throughout the 1950s, even with characters such as Bathsheba, Salome, and Sheba. In *Ben-Hur*, the seductress of Wallace's novel (Iras) is simply eliminated.

Contributing significantly to the success of the film is a colorful and tuneful score. Young's application of leitmotifs is more thorough and consistent than in the scores for earlier biblical epics and serves as an important model for *Ben-Hur*. The Samson theme (Example 4.1a), like that for Ben-Hur, has a vigorous upward leap (a minor-seventh). As is typical with melodies for action heroes, the theme is often reduced and identified with just its opening gesture.

Example 4.1a. Samson.

Example 4.1b. Miriam.

When Samson is desperate, he turns to prayer, and these moments are supported musically with a vibraphone. The use of a wavering sound to suggest a divine force echoes timbres heard in Webb's earlier score for *The Last Days of Pompeii*. A parallel moment occurs in *Ben-Hur* when Judah is denied water on his journey to the Roman fleet.

The music for Delilah and the Philistines provides substantial contrasts. Delilah's modal theme is conjunct and flows with cascading triplets. Young adds a nice touch by using Samson's head motive as an answering motive during the titles, thereby showing the entanglement of their relationship. The Philistine motive is stern and menacing, but other than this brief thematic idea and some action cues, the Philistines have little musical support. In many respects, they are the Romans of this film. They wear breastplates like Romans, they have similar weapons and antique musical instruments (tibia, harp, and kithara), and their music is limited primarily to fanfares and feast entertainment.

Perhaps the most important contribution of Young's score to the traditions of religious epics is the theme for Miriam (Example 4.1b). Young gives Miriam a dark, passionate, and anguished theme through the use of mid-register strings, multiple augmented-minor melodic intervals, minor chords, modal qualities, biting dissonances, and quick descending gestures. These features will become standard for the depiction of Jews during times of oppression (as distinct from music supporting the powerful Jewish kingdoms of David and Solomon). In this theme, Young has created a clear predecessor for Rózsa's music for Rebecca in *Ivanhoe* and Miriam in *Ben-Hur*.

Other Traditional Scores

George Duning scored the Rita Hayworth vehicle *Salome* (1953), in which the infamous seductress is given the Hollywood sympathetic treatment. Queen Herodias is shown to be the mad one (complete with the Richard Strauss *Salome* trill), and Salome is now dancing to save the life of John the Baptist. At the end, the converted Salome and Claudius are listening to Christ's Sermon on the Mount. The film hence shows three worlds: Roman, Judean, and Christian. Duning provides brass fanfares and marches for Rome, nondistinct ethnic music for Jews, and traditional triads, sometimes in parallel motion, for the followers of Christ. Several cues suggest a neo-Classic orientation, but the overall effect is similar to Young's score with its predominant lyric themes, while a few moments contain a touch of a symphonic pop style.

The Ten Commandments (1956), Cecil B. DeMille's last epic, was the culminating point of his career. He shot on location in Egypt and Mount Sinai and used 20,000 extras. Unlike the silent version of *The Ten Commandments*, this film does not focus on the Commandments (only about twenty minutes are devoted to them), but rather on Moses leading the Hebrews out of Egypt—the primary message is once again about freedom, not religion. At the center of the drama is the conflict between two men (Charlton Heston and Yul Brynner), once thought to be brothers (one of the several parallels to *Ben-Hur*).

Victor Young was set to score the film when he fell ill; he passed away shortly after the premiere. Upon Young's recommendation, DeMille hired a composer with relatively little experience, Elmer Bernstein. The task of providing music for *The Ten Commandments* was daunting. After working nearly a year on the project, Bernstein produced a Young-like score that has been described as "the crowning touch for the film."[7] Although the music is less tuneful than *Samson and Delilah*, there are multiple related themes that help unify the sprawling story. In his melodic material, Bernstein avoids ethnic clichés and suggests the time and region in a subtler manner, primarily through the use of Lombard rhythms, parlando melodies, and modality.

Alfred Newman

Alfred Newman projects an entirely different mood in the music for *David and Bathsheba* (1951). The film does not dwell on David's glories, but on one of his dark episodes—his affair with Bathsheba and the murder of her husband Uriah. This tangled story provides ambiguous moral messages about love, unfaithfulness, and religion. Capturing this discordant mood, Newman eschews the romantic style of Young for a modernistic sound. Much of the score reflects a neo-Classic character with extended modal melodies, intricate counterpoint, and woodwind solos that suggest antique timbres. Particularly intense is the extended dissonances during David's vision of the battle on Mt. Gilboa.

Newman's score for *The Robe* (1953) has a greater diversity of styles, which is largely due to multiple settings in the plot (Rome and Judea), more intense emotions (the Crucifixion), a sincere romantic relationship, and a grander production—the studio's first cinemascope feature and enhanced stereophonic sound. Much of the melodic material representing Christ and the early Christians is modeled on chant, with limited ranges and modal harmonies. The Christ/Robe theme juxtaposes unrelated major and minor triads and often employs a wordless choir. The swirling of voices heard during the opening titles and at the Crucifixion, implying the mourning of angels, takes full advantage of stereo. As in many of Newman's scores, voices play a prominent role. References to God, Christ, and heaven tend to be accompanied by this celestial sound, recalling similar moments in Newman's scores for *Wuthering Heights* and *The Song of Bernadette*. Typically, there is a triumphant choral Alleluia at the end, as Marcellus and Diane seemingly ascend to heaven.

Newman provides distinct sounds for Judea and Rome, but with a more dissonant edge than in earlier films. When Marcellus first comes to Judea, Newman evokes the musical qualities of oppressed Jews, including dark string colors, descending chantlike themes, augmented-second intervals, quick ornamental turns, and dissonant harmonies. Scenes in Rome are given little underscoring. Fanfares and festive source music are the principal musical sounds of the Empire, but Newman frequently incorporates dissonances, even in the party music. Most notable is the underlying dissonance given to Caligula's fanfare, which suggests the decadence of his character and his reign.

Other Modern Scores

In 1954, Waxman scored the sequel to *The Robe* entitled *Demetrius and the Gladiators*. He incorporated a number of Newman's themes, including those for the robe, Peter, Diane (briefly at the beginning), and some fanfare material. Waxman also retained the dissonant aura surrounding the decadent world of Caligula and Messalina. In addition to harsh fanfares, a number of cues are set for small instrumentation and exhibit a daring harmonic palette. In keeping with Newman's tradition, the wordless or humming chorus is prominent throughout and breaks into words at the end, this time a Gloria.

Waxman also scored *The Silver Chalice* in 1954. Although this film has many of the surface qualities of the standard religious epic, with settings in Antioch, Jerusalem, and Rome, historical characters such as Nero and Peter, and stock situations—Basil (Paul Newman's debut role) must decide between two women, a redeemer and a seductress—it offers a rather disjointed story with spiritual and philosophical lessons, uneven acting, and set designs that are an odd mixture of art deco, de Chirico-like fantasy backdrops, and minimalism. At times, a Bayreuth-like production is suggested, most notably with the visible stage for Peter's final monologue. Similarly, Waxman's Oscar nominated score has widely divergent qualities, including several themes and passages inspired by Wagner's *Parsifal* (an obvious connection to the story), a beautiful romantic theme in the strings, awe-inspiring brass chords, dissonant fanfares and dance music, and neo-Classic sparseness in harmony and orchestration. Much of the score is for reduced forces, often utilizing individual string instruments or a woodwind ensemble.

Mario Nascimbene is one of the earliest of a group of Italian composers to enjoy success in Hollywood. During the 1950s, he created scores for several American films, including *Alexander the Great* (1956) and *Solomon and Sheba* (1959). Jon Solomon refers to *Alexander the Great* as "one of the most historically faithful of all movies about the ancient world and perhaps one of the most intelligent, too."[8] Nascimbene supplies a unique sound ambience to the film. Forgoing the warmth and lyricism of strings, he relies largely on the martial sounds of brass and percussion. Other than brief moments of romantic expressions accompanied usually by flute and a plucked instrument (guitar and harp), the Spartan-like score is harsh and dissonant. A recurring brass fanfare is the central theme.

In a similar fashion, a solemn passage of parallel chords, predominantly in the brasses or with voices, unifies Nascimbene's score for *Solomon and Sheba*. Nascimbene provides more contrasts of timbre, largely through the addition of voices, but the brass and percussion sections remain prominent. The pounding of drums is particularly effective in the extended orgiastic dance during which Sheba (Gina Lollobrigida) seduces Solomon (Yul Brynner). Modal melodies with parallel chords and dissonances are common, while a warm, romantic mood is notably absent from this intense love story.

Unlike the Roman Empire, the fall of the Roman epic was quick. Spurred by the disastrous *Cleopatra* (1963), Hollywood's greatest era of antique epics came to an end in the mid-1960s. Alex North's score for *Spartacus* (1960) includes intense expressionism, sparse neo-classicism, and the avant-garde,[9] and his music for *Cleopatra* employs a number of dissonant cues. Nascimbene continued to create distinct scores with his music for *Barabbas* (1961), which centers on the Gregorian chant *Kyrie XI Orbis factor*. Perhaps the most intriguing "musical" sound in this film is the electronic manipulation of crowd noise as Christ is whipped near the beginning of the film. Avant-garde timbres are also heard in Toshiro Mayuzumi's music for the U.S./Italian film *The Bible: In the Beginning...* (1966). As each day passes, triads and tonality become more prominent until a lush romantic style is reached with the creation of Adam. Thereafter, the music moves easily from modern to traditional, as dictated by the plot. Just seven years after *Ben-Hur*, *In the Beginning...* marks the end of the biblical revival.

The *Ben-Hur* Synthesis

Miklós Rózsa became recognized as Hollywood's foremost composer for biblical epics. Bringing a new sense of authenticity to the genre, he viewed earlier historical films with some disdain: "There have been innumerable other historical pictures produced before *Quo Vadis*, and they were all alike in their negligent attitude toward the stylistic accuracy of their music."[10] Inspired by screenwriter Hugh Gray's extensive study of the era, Rózsa researched Greco-Roman instruments and musical fragments thoroughly prior to creating the music for *Quo Vadis* (1951). Jon Solomon observes:

> No serious composer ever became more conscious of recreating ancient Greco-Roman music in this era than Miklós Rózsa.... Rózsa's solution to the quest for musical authenticity might well be labeled the Rózsa synthesis, for he synthesized ancient musical fragments, theory, and instrumentation with melodic lines, harmonies, and orchestrations suitable to modern ears and able to evoke familiar emotional responses from modern audiences. Such a synthesis became for some composers the *sine quo non* for the scoring of "ancient" films in the fifties. It influenced even such honored film-music composers as Alfred Newman for *The Robe* (1954) and Bernard Herrmann for *Jason and the Argonauts* (1963).[11]

Rózsa's synthesis evokes an ancient age, maintains a modern musical edge, and communicates to the general public of the late 1950s. Building upon the foundations laid in his work for *Quo Vadis*, Rózsa created a pervasive antique style in *Ben-Hur* that is generated ultimately from his Hungarian nationalism. Only one cue, "Adoration of the Magi," employs conventional functional tonality (with the intent of projecting the innocence of a newborn baby). For the most part, the melodic material is based on pentatonic and modal concepts, which contribute to the perception of musical authenticity. The harmonic support for this material ranges from simple triads to complex quartal and bitonal chords, all of which can be used in parallel motion. The consistency and appropriateness in the application of these materials allow Rózsa to employ Hollywood conventions without creating a cliché-ridden, melodic score that would have been unacceptable to critics and even audiences in 1959.

The thematic material in *Ben-Hur* can be divided into three types: Roman, Jewish, and Christian. Similar distinctions were found in earlier biblical film scores, but Rózsa is more systematic. The brutality of Rome is projected with loud brass and percussion, heavy beats in duple meter, dotted rhythms, accents on weak beats, tritones, and harmonies that are dissonant or have parallel triads. Jewish and Christian themes contrast with those of Rome considerably. Both rely heavily on modal melodies supported with triads. Jewish themes, though, will have a preponderance of minor chords and sharp, biting dissonances. Christian themes are supported with major triads with little to no harmonic clashes. The artistry of Rózsa is evident in his crafting of the Esther theme, the most popular melody of the score. At once it is Jewish in its ornamental melodic style, prominent melodic fifth, and rich string timbres, it is Christian in its major triadic support and use of a motive representing Christianity, and it is linked to Ben-Hur's theme through its general contour and relationship to the cell motive.

As with the scores for *Samson and Delilah*, *Quo Vadis*, and *The Ten Commandments*, the music of *Ben-Hur* communicates with audiences largely because of its melody-dominated texture. Before analyzing the score in detail (chapter 5), an examination of the principal themes and of the general types of melodic material will illuminate the nature of Rózsa's synthesis and his keen sense of unity.

Anno Domini

The Overture commences with three resounding chords. In these strokes, Rózsa brilliantly conjures up the cold and harsh pre-Christian era and, simultaneously, establishes several of the fundamental musical qualities that underlie the score as a whole, including parallel chordal movement and dominating brass timbres. The opening theme has three parts: three chords that descend and rise a major second (Example 4.2a), a countermotive (Example 4.2b), and a three-phrase melody that grows out of the opening chords (Example 4.2c). The theme has no direct connection to specific aspects of the drama. Since it precedes the appearance of the words "Anno Domini" at the beginning of the narrative and accompanies "Anno Domini XXVI" after the prelude, Rózsa refers to it as "Anno Domini," a designation that will be retained for the sake of clarity.

Example 4.2a. Motto Chords.   **Example 4.2b. Countermotive.**

Example 4.2c. Anno Domini.

In the score, Anno Domini functions as a motto. It appears at most of the major structural moments in the film: the Overture, Prelude, and Entr'acte; the onset of the narrative; and the end of Ben-Hur's episode in Rome, just prior to his return to Judea (Table 4.1). The last unaltered statement, preceding Christ's Sermon, confirms its spiritual relationship to Jesus, and the Christ theme will assume the Anno Domini's role subsequently.

Anno Domini statements vary in mood, length, and harmony. The orchestration, dynamics, and articulation produce two divergent characters: full and sonorous or somber and reflective. For the most part, Anno Domini appears in its complete form (Example 4.2c), but two appearances, the conclusions of the Prelude and "Farewell to Rome," are limited to just the initial three chords, which shall be referred to in this analysis as the "motto chords."

Table 4.1. Anno Domini Appearances

Placement	Key	Chord	Presentation
Overture: Beginning	A	3-note quartal	Full Orchestra
Overture: End	Eb	4-note quartal	Quiet tremolos
Narrative: Beginning	C	Perfect fifth	Full Orchestra
Prelude: End	Bb	Perfect fifth	Quiet; Chords only
Farewell to Rome: End	C	Perfect fifth	Quiet; Chords only
Entr'acte: Beginning	A	3-note quartal	Full Orchestra
Entr'acte: End	F	4-note quartal	Full Orchestra
Entr'acte: End	A	4-note quartal	Full Orchestra
The Mount	F	Perfect fifth	Legato and Quiet

All statements of Anno Domini are supported with parallel harmonies. Within the narrative and for the final measures of the Prelude, the chords move in simple parallel fifths, recalling the organum technique of the early Christian church. Although historically inaccurate, the sounding of nontriadic chords suggests an ancient time and is a satisfactory compromise between authenticity and the musical expectations of audiences. Anno Domini is given a harsher harmonization at the beginning of the Overture and Entr'acte through the addition of a major second interval in the upper register (Example 4.2a), thereby creating a three-note quartal chord (E-A-D). Rózsa adds yet another pitch that produces four-note quartal harmonies in the closing measures of the Overture and Entr'acte. The barrenness and harshness of these statements stand as aural counterparts to the Christ theme, which moves with parallel major triads.

The Anno Domini also serves as a motto in the sense that it provides musical materials that are essential to the unity of the score. On the largest level, the pitches A and E in the first chord are also the opening and closing key areas of the film. More significantly, the Anno Domini suggests pentatonic pitch groupings, establishes the prevalence of modal harmony, and presents a critical melodic idea. The pitches of the first two chords (A-E-D and G-D-C) create a pentatonic scale: C, D, E, G, and A, a pitch content that is immediately reflected in the countermotive (Example 4.2b). The pitches of the initial chord prepare the listener for several of the major motives and themes that are generated from similar pitch relationships. One can take the three notes of the first chord (A, D, E), for example, and play the head motives for both Ben-Hur (Example 4.4a), with an octave displacement, and Esther (Example 4.5a), with an added decorating note.

Although the opening passage of the Overture harmonically centers on A, the melody is clearly in E Phrygian, with its characteristic half step above the central pitch (Example 4.2c).[12] Rózsa emphasizes the second degree of the mode by shifting the meter so that the F always falls on a downbeat. The three-note gesture at the beginning of the theme serves a dual purpose. The bold highlighting of the lowered leading tone immediately establishes the modality prevalent throughout the score. At the same time, it provides a germinal seed for both immediate and long-range development. The full Anno Domini theme can be heard simply as two expansions upon the three-note motive, the first with four notes and the next with five (the motive pitches are marked with the letter x in Example 4.2c).[13]

The three-note melodic motive maintains a strong presence in the Overture. During the first four measures of the Esther theme, for example, the motive occurs in the melody at the end of the second measure, and in the accompaniment three times (marked with brackets in Example 4.5a). Perhaps most significantly, Esther's countermotive introduces the three-note idea with a preparatory leap of a fourth (Example 4.5b). In this four-note form (with the added note, the pitches match those found in the first chord of the Overture), the motive resembles the second phrase of the Christ theme (the initial leap is a fourth rather than a fifth). Since this countermotive is used in the music representing both Esther and Balthazar, it provides an important musical link between these two characters and Christ.

Christ

The Anno Domini and the Christ themes serve as the musical bookends of the film. The Overture begins with Anno Domini, and the score concludes with Christ. They both have parallel harmonic movement, a limited melodic range, a suggested Phrygian mode, motto motives (marked in brackets), and a brief descending countermotive in the lower register that outlines a fifth (compare Examples 4.2b and 4.3b). The principal difference is harmony. The Christ theme, accompanied with parallel major triads, projects a sense of warmth and comfort. Hence, the film takes us on an aural journey from the harsh, cold world of conflict and hate of a pre-Christian world represented by the Anno Domini theme to the bright, joyful world of hope and love with the Christ theme.

Triadic harmony, a three-pitch head motive, and the triple meter all reflect Trinitarian symbolism in the Christ theme. In its fullest statements, the theme also has three phrases (Example 4.3a). The second expands the range upward by a step, and the third inverts the major second interval so that it ascends: B-flat–C–B-flat and C-sharp–D–

sharp–C-sharp. Suggesting hope, the theme constantly surges upward while highlighting pitches of a pentatonic scale: F, A-flat, B-flat, C, D-sharp (E-flat), and F.

Example 4.3a. Christ Theme.

Example 4.3b. Christ Countermotive.

Like Anno Domini, the Christ theme has two contrasting characters. A full orchestral statement occurs at the beginning of the Prelude, where it serves an analogous role to the Anno Domini theme at the beginning of the Overture. Glorious presentations of the Christ theme are heard only twice during the narrative, both signifying triumphs—after Jesus gives water and hope to Ben-Hur and following the climactic miracle.

The quiet statements have a shimmering quality generated by string tremolos and the wavering timbres of an electric organ and vibraphone. In this form, the theme sounds during each of the four appearances of the adult Jesus in the film: as a young man in Nazareth, when he gives water to Ben-Hur, during his Sermon, and when Ben-Hur offers him water. Similar orchestrations are heard in the moments when there is a reference to Jesus, such as Ben-Hur's recollections of his first encounter and the Balthazar and Esther references to the Prophet.

Ben-Hur and Esther

The film's leading male and female figures are given appropriately divergent thematic material: Ben-Hur's theme is virile and active, and Esther's is gentle and comforting. Yet they are clearly linked. Both are derived from pentatonic scales, and the two head motives are variations of the "cell" motive described in chapters 1 and 2;[14] Ben-Hur's theme

ascends a major second and then completes the perfect fifth, and
Esther's leaps a fifth and then falls a major second (these pitches are
marked with an "x" in Example 4.4a).

Example 4.4a. Ben-Hur Theme.

Example 4.4b. Ben-Hur Theme Altered.

The Ben-Hur theme is the most aggressive in the score. It contains
three four-measure phrases: A-B-B'. The five-note head motive features a dotted rhythm and the upward surge of an octave, recalling the
conqueror theme from Strauss's *Don Juan*, especially when the theme
is given to the French horns. The "B" phrase contains three statements
of the cell motive with a perfect fourth rather than a fifth. Each motive
returns to A-flat, and the last cadence falls to the tonic D-flat (measure
7). The third phrase is similar to "B", but uses the pitches of a new pentatonic scale centering on D-flat (C-sharp). Hence, the cadence of this
phrase arrives on G-sharp. The lack of closure for the theme as a whole
projects a sense of unpredictability, which is essential to Judah's character.

Ben-Hur's theme is presented for the first time in the Prelude,
where it receives its most complete presentation and its most characteristic key, D-flat. Within the drama, the theme reflects the condition of
Judah. In the two moments where he is invigorated—after drinking
water offered by Christ and after his return to Judea—the theme is in
the original key of D-flat, supported by cascading pentatonic harmonies. The other appearances of the theme occur in moments of stress or
sadness: desperation during his death march through the desert, just
before and during the sea battle, and in dealings with the leprosy of his
mother and sister. In these moments, the head motive is altered so that
the opening rise is a minor second (creating a tritone between the second and fifth notes), and the leap upwards is a major seventh instead of
an octave (Example 4.4b). Hence, when Judah is confident, his theme

has the strength of an octave leap. When he is unsure or under attack, the tritone and minor seventh suggests danger or pain.

Ben-Hur's theme is clearly related to the Roman themes discussed below. Messala draws our attention to Ben-Hur's natural Roman qualities: "You're like a Roman." Significantly, Ben-Hur's theme is heard primarily in his interaction with the Roman world. The last appearance of his theme occurs in the Finale, where it loses its heroic and unpredictable qualities. This is a somber final statement for the most exuberant theme in the film, and it is soon overwhelmed by the Christ theme, reflecting the critical decision of an action hero subordinating himself to Christ. During the course of the narrative, Ben-Hur has transformed from Jew, to Roman, to Christian, all of which is heard in the music.

Example 4.5a. Esther Theme.

Example 4.5b. Esther Countermotive.

Esther's theme is given the most extended playing time of any theme in the score. In its fullest form, it has an A-B-A' form, and its stability contrasts sharply with the unpredictability of Ben-Hur's theme. Esther's theme also contains an octave leap, but the mood is warm and passionate, as opposed to Ben-Hur's boldness. This character is largely generated from the lush orchestration and triadic harmony. For the most part, Esther's theme serves as a love theme, but it also signifies Esther as an individual in nonromantic situations. When it functions as a love theme, it has Rózsa's typical orchestration with a low flute register or string timbres, sometimes featuring violin and cello solos.

Hatred and Friendship

Ben-Hur's complex relationship to Messala requires two musical themes to reflect both love and hate. In order to avoid confusion with Esther's "love" theme, Ben-Hur's bond with Messala forged in their youth is referred to as "Friendship." Friendship is first heard during the Overture, and it is the primary theme underscoring the reunion of Messala and the members of the Hur family. The cue entitled "Conflict" introduces the Hatred theme, and the two themes are momentarily linked, with Hatred soon becoming dominant. As will be seen, both Hatred and Friendship feature Roman qualities.

The Hatred theme (Example 4.6) has three striking features: a strong accent on beat two of the first measure, a sharp dissonance on beat three in the second measure, and a falling tritone that is sometimes reiterated. Initially, the theme reflects Messala's revenge against Ben-Hur. But in the second half of the film, after Ben-Hur has become Roman, the theme represents Judah's hatred for Messala and Rome.

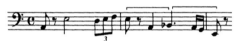

Example 4.6. Hatred.

Example 4.7a. First Phrase of Friendship.

Example. 4.7b. Finale Version of Friendship.

The Friendship theme (Example 4.7a) has some warm settings, but it also exhibits a number of disturbing qualities that foreshadow the transformation of close friends into bitter enemies; dotted rhythms, chromaticism, prominent tritones (marked with brackets), and shifting harmonies are features that are normally associated with dark characters in Rózsa's scores.

In its fullest form, the Friendship theme has two phrases, each with three motives: A-A'-B and A-A'-C. The "A" motives are two measures long. The initial "A" contains an appoggiatura-like motion followed by a dotted rhythm with a chromatic alteration and tritone. In "A'," the pitches remain the same, but the rhythm is altered. The "B" and "C" phrases have chromatic harmonies and feature a prominent melodic tritone that moves either downward (B) or upward (C). Hence the theme by its nature is transitional; rarely does a statement end in the same key that it began; the last chord of the phrase tends to be the first chord of a new phrase. This inherent modulatory character recalls the restlessness of the Ben-Hur theme, but the chromatics and tritones create a greater sense of instability.

The Friendship theme undergoes numerous transformations during the film. One of its variables is harmonization. For most statements, the melodic pitches are supported with parallel major triads, as in the Christ theme. But unlike the latter, the Friendship triads are set within other harmonic contexts, generally involving a pedal. The initial stepwise descent sounds melodically like an appoggiatura and is treated as such in several cues. But more typically, the gesture begins with a consonant chord, and the melodic descent produces harmonic tension with the underlying pedal. In the second half of the film, the death of Messala brings out a substantial transformation in the Friendship theme, where the low register of the trombones gives it a dirge quality.

The most significant modifications of Friendship occur near the end. The Hatred and Friendship themes are again linked at the beginning of the Crucifixion. At one point, the descending motive from Hatred serves as an accompaniment to the Friendship melody. Ultimately, they give way to the quiet wavers of the Christ theme, preparing us for the imminent miracle. Friendship makes one last appearance in the Finale, where its disturbing qualities have been resolved (Example 4.7b). The "A" phrases are played lyrically and without dotted-rhythms, chromatic alternations, or tritones. The unstable "B" phrase is replaced with two motives associated with Christ, the motive from his procession to Golgotha and the fall and rise of a major second. Musically, the frailties of human friendship have been resolved in Christian love.

Roman Themes

Audiences in the 1950s viewed ancient Rome with ambivalent attitudes. Although cruel and oppressive, the Roman Empire was also impressive. It had ruled the world, supplied us with numerous heroes as well as villains, and created laws, roads, and art and literature that became the basis of much of Western civilization. This duality of perception—Rome's grandeur and its harshness—resonates throughout *Ben-Hur*. Roman legions, marching with red capes and glistening armor, lend themselves to spectacular scenes with large crowds and monumental sets. Accompanying these dazzling images are numerous fanfares and five substantial marches. With a heavy percussive pulse and parallel harmonic motion in the brass, the music successfully captures both the glory and the relentless tyranny of Rome.

Rózsa reinforces this association by inserting the Hatred theme into three marches. The descending tritone cadential motion of Hatred (Example 4.6) is heard in both the initial march of Romans through Judea and Gratus's procession through Jerusalem. In the latter, the motive is reiterated eight times in succession (Example 4.8a). The opening phrase of "Parade of the Charioteers" (Example 4.8b) quotes the entire Hatred theme, but in a major key supported by parallel triads. This not only links Rome with Hatred, but also reflects Ben-Hur's emotions for Messala as they enter the arena. The appearance of Ben-Hur's heroic theme during the trio of this march further ties Judah to both Rome and Hatred.

Example 4.8a. Gratus's March.

Example 4.8b. Parade of the Charioteers.

Scoring in the Roman world is reserved for scenes of Roman conquest, conflict, and cruelty. Rózsa's harshest harmonies, generated from complex triadic and quartal chords with minor seconds, major sevenths, and tritones, are reserved for these moments. The following themes represent the Roman world and its violence. All have multiple tritones, marked with brackets. The Quintus Arrius theme (Example 4.9a) outlines a diminished triad, which suggests a dark and potentially dangerous character. The theme is heard only at sea when he is the commander, and not in Rome when he lovingly adopts Ben-Hur.

Example 4.9a. Quintus Arrius.

Example 4.9b. Roman Fleet.

Example 4.9c. Rowing.

The themes for the Roman Fleet and Rowing (Examples 4.9b and 4.9c) are related. Indeed, the Roman Fleet can be seen as an extended version of the one-measure rowing theme. The Rowing theme brilliantly reflects the physical effort of pulling oars through water, and the tritones suggest the suffering of the galley slaves. These three themes share a number of characteristics with Hatred and Friendship, including dotted rhythms, chromaticism, jagged melodic intervals, prominent tritones, accents on the second beat of the measure, and quick descending gestures. These qualities are also found in the leprosy cues and in the death marches of Ben-Hur and Christ, all of which are results of Roman cruelty.

The primary musical sounds for Rome, other than action cues, stem from source music. Among the Roman characters, only Quintus Arrius is identified musically. Notably, Messala has no theme other than Friendship and Hatred, which he shares with Ben-Hur. Substantial passages of the film dealing with Romans are devoid of music. The first extended break from scoring occurs when Messala arrives at the Roman Fortress of Antonia (4:48 in length). The next scene without music again takes place in the Fortress, just after the arrest of Ben-Hur. Once Ben-Hur becomes the Roman son of Quintus Arrius, breaks in the score become more frequent; music is absent during the meeting of Ben-Hur and Sheik Ilderim (8:13), Ben-Hur's return to the House of Hur (7:00), Ben-Hur's confrontation with Messala in the Fortress of Antonia (5:20), the Sheik's wager proposal (7:03), the race (11:13), and Ben-Hur's successive talks with Pontius Pilate and Esther (7:26). This sparseness of scoring for Roman scenes creates a sterile atmosphere that contrasts sharply with Judaic and Christian scenes.

Judaic and Christian Themes

The opposition of love and hate is reflected on a larger scale in the portrayals of two societies: Rome and Judea. Rome is depicted as an oppressive world built on violence. By contrast, Judea during the time of Christ offers peace and hope with a focus on family ties. The score has four prominent themes representing the Jewish world. The Judea theme (Example 4.10a) appears primarily at the beginning of scenes, where it identifies the locale and ethnicity of the people. The free flowing nature of the theme contrasts strikingly with the rhythmic and metric squareness of Roman marches. The initial rising fifth is a common element of Jewish themes. The interval is prominent at the beginning of the Ben-Hur and Esther themes, and it serves as the initial ranges for House of Hur and Miriam (Examples 4.10b and 4.10c).

Example 4.10a. Judea.

Example 4.10b. House of Hur.

Example 4.10c. Miriam.

The largely pentatonic Judea theme is in the Aeolian mode and has a prominent lowered-seventh cadence. The quick ornamental turns in the third and fourth measure of each phrase are common to many of the Jewish themes. Reflecting the troubled state of the region, the harmonization is often dissonant. In the Prelude, Judea is set with quartal chords and then given a bitonal countermelody. At the opening of the Ben-Hur exposition, it assimilates a heavy Roman accompaniment with plodding parallel fourths, signifying the presence of the Roman legion in the land. At the beginning of the Christ exposition, the Judea theme is played over sustained minor seconds. The resultant dissonance suggests a lament, the traditional mood in biblical epics for underscoring Jews during a time of oppression. The music projects pain, sadness, and suffering.

Similar qualities are heard in the Miriam theme, often referred to as "A Mother's Love." Like the Judea melody, Miriam is in the Aeolian mode, but it is warmer in nature because of its string timbre, triadic support, conjunct motion, and avoidance of dotted rhythms other than an expressive Scottish snap. A tinge of sadness is generated with a prevailing F-minor triad, quick biting dissonance, and frequent sighing gestures.

The fourth major Jewish theme belongs to Esther, which is discussed above. While the Esther theme shares several characteristics with Jewish themes (rising fifth, Dorian mode, ornamental flourishes), it also reflects qualities of Christian melodies. Many of these features can also be observed in Balthazar's Mixolydian theme (Example 4.11), such as triadic harmony, warm orchestrations, and an embedded statement of the motto motive (marked with a bracket). Similar musical qualities are sustained in other Christian scenes, most notably the Nativity and Christ's Sermon. The themes for Esther and Balthazar also share the same countermotive (Example 4.5b), which clearly links the two figures that are the strongest advocates for Christ in the film.

Example 4.11. Balthazar.

Reflecting techniques of epic scoring established by Max Steiner in *Gone With the Wind*, Rózsa sustains an overall freshness of musical material in *Ben-Hur* through the number and variety of easily recognizable thematic ideas. Rózsa's craftsmanship can be seen in the continuity created by the consistent application of historical and ethnic qualities and the clarity of the complex thematic interrelationships. Building from these materials, Rózsa also develops a large-scale musical structure, as detailed in chapter 5.

5

AN ANALYSIS OF THE SCORE

Rózsa faced numerous challenges in composing *Ben-Hur*. Perhaps the greatest of these was to unify such a diverse and lengthy score. His success in this regard is due in part to the overall antique style and the manipulation of thematic material (see chapter 4). In addition, Rózsa created a successful large-scale structure that can be observed on several levels.

Rózsa takes advantage of the plot's ABA structure (Judea, Exile, Judea) to create a tripartite musical form. All of the major themes other than Hatred are presented during the double exposition, and each, including Hatred, reappears in its original or most recognizable key after Ben-Hur returns to Judea (Table 5.1). The middle portion of the film has several Roman themes that are not heard in the outer sections, and it contains the most unstable and developmental cues of the film (desert march and sea battle). It would be inappropriate to equate this score with a symphonic sonata form, but many of the same principles are applied, giving the music a great sense of cohesion.

Table 5.1. Thematic Reprises

Theme	Original Key	Reprise Key	Reprise Cue
Ben-Hur	Db	Db	Judea
Balthazar	D	D	Ilderim
Esther	Bb, F, C	F, C, Bb	Judea, Hur, Entr'acte
Judea	A	A	Entr'acte
Anno Domini	A	A	Entr'acte
Hatred	A	A	Frustration
Miriam	F	F	Return
Christ	Bb	Bb	Miracle

There are also a number of individual key associations. The clearest is D-flat/C-sharp for Ben-Hur, the key center for the initial presentation of this theme in the Overture and for many of its appearances in the narrative. Despite this prominence, the key does not achieve a structural status, but functions as a local signifier of the protagonist. The only person to share this pitch center is Quintus Arrius, who becomes Judah's father by adoption. Another prominent pitch center is A, which is heard with the Anno Domini statements at the beginning of the Overture and Entr'acte, with the majority of Roman marches, and with the Hatred theme. This association suggests that A represents the harshness of the pre-Christian world. Two other notable key centers are D, which is Balthazar's principal key and the pitch for Christ's birth and procession to Calgary, and E, which is used for Leprosy.

On the largest level, we have noted that the score begins in A (pre-Christian world) and ends gloriously in E (Christian world), completing the perfect fifth that seems to represent man's goodness. In between, the score moves freely through numerous key areas, thereby avoiding monotony. But the length of several pitch centers after the intermission suggests structural significance. The Entr'acte, which begins and ends in A, is followed by Circus music in A. The span of this tonal center in the score is matched only by Christ's lengthy procession to Calgary in D, a pitch center that continues into the Crucifixion scene. The other pitch to achieve structural prominence is E, the final key of the score. Hence, we are left at the end of the film with three primary key areas—A, D, and E. As for this significance, one needs only to recall the three pitches of the first chord in the score, shown in Example 4.2a.

These observations provide a framework for the detailed analysis that follows. Because of the length of the score, the scope has been limited. During the course of composition and recording, substantial sections of original music were revised or simply cut. For the sake of clarity and the desire to limit the size of this chapter, this analysis will focus on the music as heard in the completed film. Readers wanting details on the manuscript and the process that led to the final product are directed to Ralph Erkelenz's thorough five-part study of the score published in *Pro Musica Sana.*[1]

In keeping with this concentration on the film version of the music, a list of cues as they appear in the manuscript has been omitted, as this would introduce numerous side issues. Cue titles will be referenced in the analyses for those that can gain access to the score. Since numerous cues appear consecutively and important musical thoughts begun in one cue are often completed in another, the discussion of the musical discourse as perceived by the listener will take precedence over boundaries set by cues in the score.

The Christ Exposition

Following a substantial overture, the narrative presents a simple and relatively brief depiction of the birth of Jesus. At the opening, we observe Joseph and Mary passing through Jerusalem on their journey to Bethlehem, as the narrator (Balthazar) describes the troubled times for Judea. These are the only spoken words in this exposition; the remaining two scenes are tableaus of the North Star and the Nativity. The cues "Anno Domini," "Star of Bethlehem," and "Adoration of the Magi" coincide with these three scenes.

By the end of the exposition, Rózsa has introduced all of the major themes in the film with the exceptions of Ben-Hur and Hatred. The Overture contains a medley of themes from the richly melodic score, the Jerusalem segment centers on the Judea theme and briefly previews the Christ theme, and the vision of the North Star is accompanied by Balthazar's theme. The only significant nonrecurring material is the gentle vocal pastorale that underscores the Nativity. The joyful mood and major harmony of the last two scenes stand in contrast to the dissonance and predominant minor harmonies of the first scene and to several passages of the Overture. This shift from harshness to joyfulness foreshadows the musical progression of the film as a whole.

Overture

The Overture has a simple structure. Framed by Anno Domini, four themes associated with Judah Ben-Hur are heard in succession. Judea sets the location, and the succeeding themes represent Judah's closest relationships: his romantic interest, his mother (family), and his childhood friend (Table 5.2). More detailed discussions of these themes are in the thematic overview in chapter 4.

The Anno Domini and Judea sections are linked together; they share the same pitch center, feature modal melodic material, and contain similar quartal harmonies. Immediately following the eight-measure statement of Anno Domini, Judea appears in two contrasting settings, neither of which recurs in the narrative. The first takes the character of an exotic dance, complete with a sprightly woodwind melody, echo imitations, and a rhythmic pizzicato ostinato. The initial harmony, a four-pitch quartal chord (B, E, A, D), contains all three pitches of the first Anno Domini chord (see Example 4.2a). Just prior to the end of the statement, the harmony moves to an imperfect five-pitch quartal chord (E-flat, A, D, G, C),[2] and the resultant minor-second dissonance resolves at the cadence.

Table 5.2. Overture Themes

Theme	Measures	Key
Anno Domini	1-8	A
Judea	9-58	A
Esther	59-102	Bb
Miriam	103-128	F
Friendship	129-170	C, F, Db, Bb, Eb
Anno Domini	171-182	Eb

The second statement of Judea is darker and more disturbing. The melody is given in the lower register of the strings (played *sul G*) and is supported with chromatically shifting harmonies. A haunting countermelody creates a striking passage of bitonality.[3] While the principal melody remains in A, the countermelody (Example 5.1) initially centers on E and maintains an independent pitch center throughout. This secondary melodic idea is supported with parallel harmonies beginning with a three-pitch quartal chord (D, A, E), which matches the opening harmony for Anno Domini. Indeed, the first three chords and the cadence of the countermelody (marked with brackets) are essentially identical to the motto chords of Anno Domini (Example 4.2a).

Example 5.1. Judea Countermelody in the Overture.

The Esther and Miriam themes are the heart of the Overture. With triadic harmonies, string-dominated orchestrations, regular phrase lengths, and A-B-A structures, they generate a warm, stable character that contrasts with the harsher qualities in the outer portions of the Overture. These two themes represent pure love, but their tones differ. Esther's theme also symbolizes the emergence of Christianity, and the expansive upward leaps in her theme, including a climactic octave in the third phrase, suggest both passion and joy. The first phrase of Miriam's theme introduces qualities associated with Jews in a time of oppression (see chapter 4)—a rich low-string register, prevailing minor chords, and a descending sighing gesture (measures two and four). The second phrase of the Miriam theme initiates a passage of two-part counterpoint. The violins play the principal melody, which predominantly descends, while the lower strings continue with a variation of the first phrase; the two lines generally move in contrary motion. The B section continues with this melodic interplay and projects the dual sense of steadfast love and sacrifice.

The Friendship theme shares several features in common with the melodies for Esther and Miriam, including an A-B-A form, string timbres, and triadic harmonies. But Friendship also introduces some unsettling qualities with its dotted rhythms, tritones, and frequent modulations. This shift in mood leads directly into the subdued final statement of the Anno Domini. Ultimately marked "Molto Tranquillo," Anno Domini is played quietly with tremolo strings, woodwinds, French horns, and percussion. The final pitch center of E-flat forms a tritone with the opening A. Throughout the film, the tritone symbolizes man's failing and the harshness of the pre-Christian world, whereas the perfect fifth represents man's strength through goodness and Christ. The tritone relationship of the Overture is ultimately resolved at the end of the film, where E major rounds out the perfect fifth relationship.

Narrative

The return of the Anno Domini theme announces the beginning of the narrative. Its full symphonic orchestration recalls the opening of the Overture, but the pitch center is now C, and the quartal chords of the Overture are replaced with simple open fifths. As in the Overture, the Judea theme follows immediately in the same pitch area. Rózsa gives Judea a biting minor-second accompaniment and adds a descending countermotive that suggests a lament (Example 5.2). This setting reflects the state of Jerusalem, "the troubled heart of their land," under Roman occupation.

Example 5.2. Judea Countermotive in "Anno Domini."

The playing of the Judea theme is interrupted briefly at the mention of the Fortress of Antonia, when a brass fanfare with parallel triadic harmonies suggests the military power of Rome. With the following reference to the temple, a wordless male choir intones a chantlike phrase in the Phrygian mode, using the pitches of the preceding fanfare. After these diversions, the Judea theme resumes. Near the end of the cue, the Christ theme makes its initial appearance, quietly underscoring the vision of the expectant Mary and the narrator's reference to the Redeemer. Beneath the last chord of the Christ theme, the Judea countermotive returns in a low register, reminding us that Christ was born into a troubled Jewish world.

The "Star of Bethlehem" presents the Balthazar theme in its full A-B-A form. In keeping with the traditions of biblical epics, the cue includes a wordless choir that suggests the host of angels celebrating this event. Similar to the Esther theme, Balthazar's modal melody (Hypolydian on D) has prominent lowered-seventh degree cadences, moves in simple four-measure phrases, and is supported with triadic harmonies. Further linking these two themes is the common four-note countermotive heard in the Overture (Example 4.5b). Throughout, the triadic harmonies are enriched with cross-relations,[4] imitation, and contrary motion.

The harmonic shift from D to F at the beginning of the "Adoration of the Magi" creates another prominent cross-relation. This tableau contains the most conventional music in the score; the functional harmony, homophonic texture, and simple melody project childlike innocence. For the most part, the melody has four-measure phrases that are extended by two beats in order to incorporate echoing motives, including a half-step descent that suggests the bleating of an animal. The tune is clearly tied to Balthazar's theme, as both begin with identical pickups and have similar timbres—lyric strings, solo woodwinds that contribute to the pastoral character, and (beginning with the B section) a wordless choir. With the return of Balthazar's theme, reflecting his presence at the Nativity, the harmonies shift from F to D-flat, once again requiring chromatic adjustments. The new pitch area also prepares the listener for the imminent arrival of Ben-Hur's key in the Prelude.

The Ben-Hur Exposition

The action in the Ben-Hur exposition takes place twenty-six years later. As in the Christ exposition, the narrative has three parts: the march of the Roman legion through Nazareth, the meeting of Messala and Sextus, and the reunion of Messala and Ben-Hur. Four fundamental ideas necessary to the plot are established: the basic conflict between the adult

Christ and Rome, the power and arrogance of Rome, the friendship between Messala and Ben-Hur, and the seeds of their falling out.

There are several musical parallels with the Christ exposition: the
narrative is preceded by a musical introduction ("Prelude"), the Judea
theme initiates the narrative portion, and the Christ theme is heard quietly during the first scene. The most important new melody is the presentation of the Ben-Hur theme during the Prelude.

Fanfare

Throughout the film, the conflict between Christ and Rome is depicted
musically with loud, obtrusive Roman fanfares following or interrupting
gentle Christ cues. The first example of this occurs just prior to the prelude. The Christ exposition ends with the quiet sounding of a shofar, an
instrument made from an animal's horn and used to announce important
Jewish events. An instant later, a brass fanfare blares out, aurally thrash-
ing any sense of peace associated with the birth of Jesus. This stark contrast can be linked to the traditional symbolism voiced perhaps most
clearly in Thomas Inces's *Civilization* (1916), in which the bugles of
war give way to the shepherd's horn. In this instance, of course, the roles
are reversed.

Within eight measures, Rózsa moves from the simplicity of birth to
the grandeur of Christ via a brief, well-crafted Roman fanfare. The first
four measures (Example 5.3) recall the opening of the Overture with its
pentatonic pitches and parallel fourths. At the same time, this passage
prepares the listener for the arrival of the Ben-Hur theme; all of these
pitches can be found in the accompaniment to the initial statement of
Ben-Hur, and, by rearranging the first four notes of the fanfare (moving
the first note to the third), you can reproduce the pitches of Ben-Hur's
head motive (Example 4.4a).

Example 5.3. Fanfare Opening.

The fanfare's emphasis on the interval of a minor third is also significant. The first four measures emphasize B-flat and D-flat (measure
two of Example 5.3), which are the principal key areas of the Prelude as
a whole. The minor third also prepares the listener for the arrival of the
Christ theme, which primarily falls within that interval. The fifth mea-

sure of the fanfare, coinciding with the appearance of the title, dramatically shifts from three-part imitation to a chordal texture with parallel chords beginning on an A-flat triad. With the return of B-flat at the end, the fanfare has moved from B-flat – A-flat – B-flat. Hence, the fanfare is simply an elaborate variation of the motto chords at the beginning of Anno Domini, which descend a major second and return.

Prelude

The Prelude presents four themes: Christ, Ben-Hur, Esther, and Anno Domini. The Christ theme fills the same introductory role in the Prelude as Anno Domini did in the Overture. With brass and tubular bells, the theme suggests the eventual triumph of Christ. At the conclusion of the film, this theme will return in the same key (B-flat) and with a similar orchestration. The Christ theme enters with the appearance of the words: "A Tale of the Christ." During the Overture, the screen image is taken from Michelangelo's "The Creation of Adam" on the Sistine Chapel ceiling. The close-up of the hand of God giving life to Adam is a clear reference to the Old Testament. During the Prelude, the full fresco is shown, which, according to some interpreters, contains the image of the unborn Jesus, an appropriate backdrop to the full orchestral setting of the Christ theme. The theme is presented with all three of its three-measure phrases, as described in chapter 4. The cadential phrase modulates to D-flat, the key of Ben-Hur.

The Ben-Hur theme dominates the Prelude. The exuberance of the theme is generated in part from its accompaniment, which features cascading pentatonic scales in contrary motion at four different rhythmic levels. This wash of sound is supported with sustained brass chords and bells. The first two phrases of the melody are also pentatonic, but they derive their pitches from a scale (G-flat, A-flat, B, D-flat, and E-flat) set a major second below that of the accompaniment (A-flat, B-flat, D-flat, E-flat, and F). Removing the common pitches of the two scales results in seven notes that form a Mixolydian mode on D-flat. With the arrival of the third phrase (B'), the harmony intensifies by shifting to A and introducing minor-second dissonances. Hence, the final phrase of the theme is not cadential, but open-ended. Although D-flat is clearly the central key of the theme, the harmonic shifting touches upon a number of divergent areas: D-flat, A, G-sharp, D-flat, F, A-flat, B, and F-sharp.

The appearance of Esther's theme is limited to just the reprise statement of the "A" phrase. It is set in B-flat, the same key center as in the Overture, and the orchestration and harmonization are nearly identical to the earlier statement. One notable change is the initial pickup—a rising major second instead of the fourth. With this simple modification, Esther's theme links aurally to the previous Ben-Hur theme, which also begins with a step ascent. A modulation returns to the pitch center to D-flat for one last statement of Ben-Hur, which in turn twists back to B-flat for the closing Anno Domini.

Nazareth

The Ben-Hur exposition begins with a Roman legion led by Messala and Drusus marching through Nazareth on their way to Jerusalem. Two cues separated by dialogue underscore this scene, "Marcia Romana" and "Spirit and Sword." The film's first Roman march, which is heard in both cues, exhibits many of the basic qualities of the Roman sound: emphatic pulses, predominant brass and percussion, dotted rhythms, accents on weak beats, and parallel harmonies. The texture has three distinct parts: a two-measure bass ostinato, a reiterated pedal with the pitches F and G, and a melody that extends sixteen measures in four-measure phrases. Both the ostinato and melody are supported with parallel fifths.

The Judea theme, which frames "Marcia Romana," maintains its chameleon nature, as it assimilates the ostinato accompaniment of the Roman march. In keeping with the general martial character, the free flowing rhythms heard in Judea's earlier statements are now more measured. Following the dialogue break, the image of Christ is scored with two quiet statements of his first phrase (in F and then G) separated by the countermotive. As at the beginning of the Prelude, the gentleness of Christ's theme is abruptly interrupted with the return of the forceful Roman march.

Fortress of Antonia

Messala's arrival at the Roman fortress is announced by an obligatory Roman fanfare. Once the story moves inside, music is largely absent; the dialogue between Messala and Sextus has no scoring. Messala shows no sign of warmth or compassion until he sees Ben-Hur. At this point, he moves between childlike giddiness and masterful manipulation, which Rózsa captures in the cue entitled "Friendship."

The psychological complexity of the relationship between Ben-Hur and Messala is reflected in the fantasy-like treatment of the Friendship theme (Example 4.7a). Some statements suggest the love of two friends, and others foreshadow their imminent falling out. Initially, the theme is limited to "A" phrases, but it expands to its full A-B-A length as the friends embrace. During this portion of the cue, the key areas move through the circle of fifths: D, G, C, and F. The warmth of the strings, the quiet dynamics, and the relatively consonant harmonies reflect the genuine happiness of their reunion. As they talk of a toast, the music softens further with the addition of the oboe and clarinet and the replacement of the dotted rhythms with even eighths in both the melody and countermotive. The harmonic movement becomes less systematic, as the key centers of E, D, C, A, B, A-flat, and D-flat precede the arrival of F-sharp with the spear throwing.

At this point, the entrance of brass, the clipped dotted rhythms, and harsher harmonies sound ominous. As Judah acknowledges their differences ("You're a Roman"), Rózsa gives the cue a poignant quality, making the first note of the theme an appoggiatura and assigning the melody to the low register of the violas. This mood is sustained until they enter Messala's quarters, which Ben-Hur describes as "a bit grim." Messala disagrees, noting that it is "austere, virtuous, Roman." In keeping with such qualities, music is absent. The Friendship theme reappears briefly at the end of the scene when they drink a toast. This cue begins in E and moves to C for the transition to the House of Hur cue.

House of Hur

The first set of complications occurs at the House of Hur, where we see the high position and wealth of the Hur family. In successive scenes, Ben-Hur develops new relationships with childhood acquaintances; Ben-Hur's friendship with Messala deteriorates into hatred, and his relationship with the slave Esther ignites into love. Contradicting his earlier proclamation "Down Eros, Up Mars," Judah has chosen the path of love that will lead symbolically to Christian redemption. Fate, however, brings down Ben-Hur's world and sends him on an improbable journey before that goal is attained. Heard for the first time in this section are the House of Hur and Hatred themes. In addition, a Roman march adumbrates the imminent downfall of the Hur family.

Ben-Hur and Messala

The deterioration of Ben-Hur's relationship with Messala can be heard in the contrasting cues titled "House of Hur" and "Conflict." The first reflects the happiness of Messala's reunion with the Hur family. It begins with a two-measure statement of the House of Hur motive in C (Example 4.10b). From this point, the Hur theme becomes a countermotive to the "A" phrase of Friendship. Initially, the oboe plays a leisurely, ornamented version of Friendship in C-sharp (the enharmonic equivalent to Ben-Hur's primary key of D-flat). When Miriam recalls that they "were good boys," the dotted rhythms return, as the Friendship theme assumes its most recognizable form. Despite some modulations, the cue concludes in C-sharp, creating a sense of relative stability. Rounding out the cue, a variation of the House of Hur theme decorates the final chord.

Example 5.4a. Opening Chord for "Hatred."

Example 5.4b. Friendship Countermotive Derived from Hatred.

"Conflict" contains the initial presentation of the Hatred theme (Example 4.6), which alternates twice with statements of Friendship. The cue begins after Ben-Hur's passionate declaration that he is against Messala. The theme enters in its most recognizable key center, A. The intensity of his anger is supported by the Roman qualities of the theme (see chapter 4) and by a stinger chord that combines the interval of a fourth, E-A, with a G-minor triad (Example 5.4a). The immediate repetition of the Hatred theme is played in the strings with parallel fourths. The melody is in G, but the underlying harmony is a sustained A-flat-major triad, which ensures multiple half-step dissonances.

At this point, Messala leaves the house, and a somber statement of the Friendship theme reflects the end of their childhood relationship. Underlying the theme is a new countermelody derived from the cadence of the Hatred theme (Example 5.4b). As Ben-Hur explains to his family what has just happened, two additional statements of Hatred appear in the same key areas as the beginning of the cue, but with more subdued harmonizations. As the family sits to eat, Friendship returns quietly, now decorated by the Judea ornamental turn (reflecting the Jewish rituals seen as they begin to eat).

Ben-Hur and Esther

Ben-Hur soon meets the adult Esther. She asks permission to marry another man, but she obviously loves Ben-Hur, a feeling that is quickly
reciprocated. The Esther theme is heard continuously through three
overlapping cues that extend for nearly seven minutes (Table 5.3).
"Esther" begins when Judah first sees her on the stairs. Played by the
strings, the initial presentation of the full theme is in F. The setting is
similar to the versions in the Overture and Prelude, but the echoes in the
"A" section are replaced by threefold imitations of the cadential turn.
This simplification allows the accompaniment's three-note Anno
Domini motto to be heard more distinctly.

Table 5.3. The Esther Theme

Cue	Theme	Key
Esther	ABA	F
	Free	
	A	Ab
Love Theme	ABBA	C
Ring for Freedom	Free	
	A	Eb
	Free	
	A	C#

When the scene changes to the upstairs room, the "Love Theme"
cue begins with another complete statement of the theme. Here, Rózsa
blurs the distinction between source music and scoring. A solo alto flute
with a harp accompaniment plays the theme in C. The timbre suggests a
performance of unseen house musicians, but the cue expands into orchestral scoring with the arrival of the "B" section.

As the romance intensifies, "Ring for Freedom" introduces a violin
solo, which leads to a melodic statement that remains in C, but is supported with D-flat chords, the key that represents Ben-Hur. After some
chromatic shifting, harmony and melody converge briefly on B-flat,
Esther's original key. This gives way to an extended E-flat statement,
with a solo cello playing the melody and a solo violin echoing the cadential sixteenths. As they kiss, another quick modulation brings the
theme to C-sharp with a passionate new countermelody in the violins.
The music remains in Ben-Hur's key at the end of the sequence, as he
touches Esther's slave ring on his finger.

Accident and Aftermath

The tenderness and passion of the love segment give way to loud percussive sounds. The Gratus's March is the harshest of the five Roman marches in the film. The march recalls the Hatred theme with its pitch center (A), second-beat accents, and repetitions of a descending tritone, which is a variation of the Hatred cadential motive (Example 4.8a). This tritone gesture is heard eight times in succession during the march. Rózsa's performance direction is "energico e brutale." The mood suggests the resentment of the Jews watching the procession, but the music is also timed so that the second playing of the reiterated tritones coincides with the view of Messala passing the House of Hur, refusing to look at either Judah or Tirzah.

Typical of scenes dominated by Romans, the accident that leads to Judah's arrest has no musical accompaniment. The next cue, "Reminiscences," follows immediately after the arrest and is one of the most poignant in the film. Having condemned Judah and his family, Messala ascends to the rooftop where he used to play as a child. A tranquillo setting of Friendship suggests memories of a happier time. Set primarily for oboe, clarinet, and strings, the cue moves through the circle of fifths. As he stands at the spot of the accident, a perfect fourth F–B-flat is combined with an A-major triad, creating the plaintive sound of a major seventh. At this moment, the descending tritone countermotive first heard after their argument (Example 5.4b) returns. Several mild accents underscore his realization that the falling tile was an accident, but the low register and dissonances suggest that this will make no difference. Messala is no longer a child; he is Roman.

Inside the walls of the Antonio Fortress, music is once again largely withheld. Music returns only after Judah vows revenge. The "Vengeance" cue again juxtaposes the Hatred and Friendship themes. The first two notes of the Hatred theme, C and G, clash with a D-flat and A-flat in the harmony. Sharp accents, biting dissonances, a heavy low register, and descending tritones mark this bleak moment for Ben-Hur. After a second statement of Hatred on F, the Friendship theme emerges as Judah walks under the arch where they had earlier thrown spears. Bitonal chords, beginning with G major over A-flat major second-inversion, reflect the irony of the moment. The dark register continues in a brief cue entitled "Prison," underscoring the arrival of Simonides and Esther. A final statement of Hatred follows the imprisonment of Simonides. The theme appears at the same pitch level as its original presentation, but the first note has been raised from an A to a B-flat, creating another melodic tritone. Written at beginning of the cue entitled "Desert," this segues directly into the desert march.

Exile

The next set of complications contains some of the most intense music of the film. Tested by fire (burning sun) and water (galley slave), Ben-Hur survives (symbolized by being offered water by two different men) and begins a series of reversals that will eventually lead him back to Judea as a Roman citizen. The music for this portion of the film is dominated by Roman qualities, reflecting the brutality of their world. The new thematic material introduced in this portion of the film—Roman Fleet, Quintus Arrius, Rowing, and Pirates—is limited to the scenes at sea.

Desert

The march to the sea is set with three consecutive cues: "Desert," "Exhaustion," and "The Prince of Peace." The music for the desert march suggests the prisoner's tortuous footsteps with slow, ponderous accents on the first and third beats of every measure; chromaticism and dissonances (often imperfect quartal chords) project their agony. Initially, the music moves in three-measure phrases, in which the third measure is a repetition of the first (Example 5.5a). Since the march immediately follows a statement of Hatred, it is easy to connect the two; both have a triplet rise and a descent of a large, disjointed interval (here a major seventh). The desert march also prepares the listener for the appearance of Ben-Hur's theme in "Exhaustion," where the first interval is a chromatic half step, and the octave leap is altered to a major seventh. Further linking the march to Ben-Hur is the central pitch, C-sharp, which clashes with a pedal D. Upon the repetition of the three-measure unit, the melody, now with parallel tritones, moves to Ben-Hur's key of D-flat.

Example 5.5a. Desert March.

With the image of Judah staggering through the desert, a rising sequence moves to A-flat. A new thematic idea reiterates an A-natural (Example 5.5b), creating a constant minor-second clash with the prevailing harmony. As a prisoner dies, the march theme returns forcefully in the trombones. The music soon fades, and the theme sinks into a lower register. With the presence of Christ implied by the sounds of a carpenter, the meter changes to triple, and a new rising countermelody suggests hope.

Example 5.5b. Desert Motive.

In "Exhaustion," Ben-Hur and the other prisoners arrive at a well in Nazareth, where a new chromatic figure containing another prominent triplet rhythm is heard (Example 5.6a). The idea rises in pitch and picks up an imitative echo at the interval of a tritone. Chromaticism, dissonances, and increasing dynamics suggest Judah's desperation. This section climaxes with the entrance of the distorted Ben-Hur theme (Example 4.4b) and a new countermotive in the violins (Example 5.6b). Centering on a descending pentatonic triplet figure, this gesture is common in the action music of this film.[5] Initially in F, the harmony shifts to Ben-Hur's D-flat as he falls and asks God for help.

Example 5.6a. Desperation.

Example 5.6b. Desperation Countermotive.

Example 5.6c. Roman Guard.

"The Prince of Peace" begins as Christ gives water to Ben-Hur. The gentle version of the Christ theme appears in F with all three of its phrases. When the Roman leader intrudes, the key center shifts a tritone to C-flat. The Roman Guard melody (Example 5.6c), however, remains in F, creating a tritone dissonance with its harmony. The confrontation between the guard and Jesus prompts a canon based on the Guard theme with the voices separated by a tritone, C and G-flat.

When Jesus wins the standoff, the first phrase of the Christ theme returns in F. Refreshed, Judah walks away with an invigorated statement of his unaltered theme in D-flat, which includes the original pentatonic accompaniment. These two pitch centers, D-flat and F, theoretically resolve the prior C and G-flat tritone. The second phrase of the Christ theme and its countermotive conclude the cue, now played with the force of the full orchestra in E-flat.

Sea

Once again, the joyful sounds of Christ are interrupted with that of raw Roman power. In the next scene, Quintus Arrius becomes commander of the Roman ship in which Ben-Hur is serving as a galley slave. The unfolding relationship between the two is supported with five musical segments: "Roman Galley," "Salute for Arrius," "Quintus Arrius," "The Galley," and "Rest."

Appropriately, "Roman Galley" mimics "Mars, the Bringer of War" from Gustav Holst's *The Planets*. Rózsa employs a simple rhythmic ostinato consisting of an eighth and three sixteenths, a standard rhythm for Roman fanfares. Like the melodic material of Holst, the Roman Fleet theme (Example 4.9b) appears in the baritone register (French horns, trombones, and violas), immediately ascends and lingers on a tritone, and continues to surge upward, rising to an augmented octave and eventually a tenth.

The Quintus Arrius theme (Example 4.9a) is first heard when the commander talks of their mission. It is given in C-sharp and supported with parallel first-inversion triads over ominous descending chromatic lines. Following the rowing test ("The Galley"), both the Roman Fleet and Arrius themes return in "Rest." The Arrius theme is still in C-sharp when Ben-Hur enters the commander's quarters. The colorful orchestration here includes tremolos and muted brass, and the ominous mood suggests the danger posed by Ben-Hur's presence while Arrius sleeps. The Arrius motive shifts to the low strings in pizzicato before the startled commander wakes to a G-minor chord with an added C-sharp.

One of the most memorable musical ideas in the score is the Rowing motive. Heard initially at the end of "Roman Galley" and more extensively in "The Galley," the one-measure ostinato (Example 4.9c) shares its general shape with the Roman Fleet theme (see discussion in chapter 4). In its rise of a fifth and fall of a fourth, two tritones are created. This, combined with trombone glissandos and the pounding of the hortator, generates an aural equivalent to the physical effort of rowing. Two other ideas build tension along with the primary ostinato. The violas and horns have an intermittent ostinato of their own with glissandos that outline a diminished triad, which creates yet another tritone (Example 5.7). In addition, the trumpets, violins, and woodwinds play a repeated figure in parallel fifths that recalls a motive heard during Ben-Hur's desert march (Example 5.5b).

Example 5.7. Rowing Countermotive.

In the dramatic rowing test ("The Galley"), the tempo of the ostinato matches the increasing speed of the rowing: normal, battle, attack, and ramming speeds. The cue begins on C, and the material is initially limited to the three motives described above. At attack speed, tension escalates dramatically; the pitch center shifts to A-flat, the ostinato of Example 5.7 is given parallel first-inversion minor triads, woodwinds play trills, brass instruments enter on beats two and four with reiterated first-inversion diminished-major seventh chords, and the French horns eventually add ascending rips. Ramming speed brings the fullest orchestration with a new brass repeating dotted rhythm in parallel fifths and a descending figure moving primarily in parallel major seconds on beats two and four. The passage closes in F.

Battle

The battle features a succession of cues entitled "Battle Preparations (Parts I and II)," "The Pirate Fleet," "Attack!," "Ramming Speed," and "Battle (Parts I and II)." In "Battle Preparations" (Table 5.4), Rózsa previews the major thematic material that is heard during the confrontation. The menacing Pirate theme is introduced in a low register and features a quick chromatic descent on the downbeat of its second measure (Example 5.8). Initially, the theme is heard over wavelike chromatic figures with trumpet calls resonating in the background, reflecting the commander's order to signal the Roman fleet. A cut to the galley shows

Quintus Arrius putting on his armor. In the galley, we hear the Roman themes—Rowing, Roman Fleet, and Quintus Arrius—and the Ben-Hur theme (with the major seventh leap). The Christ theme also appears briefly, suggesting that a spiritual hand is guiding the fate of Ben-Hur.

Example 5.8. Pirate Theme from "The Pirate Fleet."

Table 5.4. "Battle Preparations"

Action	Music
View of Pirate Fleet	Pirate theme; battle calls
Arrius descends into galley	Rowing theme with war sounds
Slaves withdraw oars	Quick descending figures
Slaves chained to oars	Variation of Roman Fleet over chromatic bass
Arrius orders Ben-Hur un-chained	Quintus Arrius theme with parallel triads
Ben-Hur unchained	Two-part counterpoint with a variation of the Roman Fleet theme
Ben-Hur is puzzled	Ben-Hur theme in E
Ben-Hur recalls Christ	Christ theme in A
Rowing resumes	Rowing theme ("The Pirate Fleet" beginning)

The two fleets engage in battle during "The Pirate Fleet." The conflict is represented in the music through contrasting timbres, counterpoint, and tonality. By this time, Rózsa has established two opposing timbres: trumpets represent Romans, and French horns and low brasses Pirates. Once the six-measure Pirate theme has been stated, the low brasses play the dominant-seventh chord of B (F-sharp), which clashes with the trumpet C-major triad (m. 14 of the cue). Two-part imitation ensues, pitting the trumpets against French horns. The chromatic waves continue in the strings, and the woodwinds and harp mimic the flight of firebombs with chromatic flourishes. Nine measures later, the brasses join in a bitonal fanfare (Example 5.9). The trombones initially play a first inversion B-major chord (B is still the Pirate key area at this point), and the trumpets have a G-major triad. The middle notes of the respective triads are identical, but the other pitches contain two half-step clashes that sound in each succeeding chord.

Example 5.9. Bitonal Fanfare.

During the initial stages of the battle, the Rowing theme interrupts the action music four times. The first follows a moment where the slaves withdraw their oars to the same descending figures heard just prior to the battle (noted in Table 5.4). The Rowing theme then resumes along with a variation of the Roman Fleet theme in counterpoint. The second entrance coincides with a cut to Ben-Hur; Rowing is presented in his key, C-sharp, while battle sounds continue in the winds. The third statement follows the commander's spotting of a vulnerable pirate ship (this moment brings out the Pirate theme). With the order for ramming speed, Rowing appears in C at an accelerated tempo. The temporary victory is marked by a return of the Roman Fleet theme. A sighting of a pirate ship that is about to ram into the commander's vessel brings out the fourth Rowing entrance; the slower tempo suggests the inevitable impact.

The frantic action both above and below deck marks the turning point in the film for Ben-Hur. Immediately after the last Rowing theme, a variation of one of the Rowing countermotives (Example 5.7) emerges with parallel triadic support over descending chromatics (marked "Pandemonium"). The attack by the pirate ship prompts a two-part canon with the Pirate theme, separated by the interval of a thirteenth. Initially the canonic voices are separated by two beats, but the separation soon expands to four beats. The hand-to-hand fighting brings out more syncopation and the reduction of the Rowing countermotive to just three notes in parallel bitonal chords (measures 2 and 3 in Example 5.10) and a variation of the Pirate theme.

Example 5.10. Hand-to-Hand Fighting.

Ben-Hur's modified theme is first heard over an A pedal as he begins to rescue other slaves. After this point, his head motive becomes
one additional motive tossed around during the chaos of fighting and
sinking. The music surges upward when Ben-Hur makes the critical decision to climb to the main deck. Amidst battle music, he saves Arrius
by spearing a pirate and then by pulling him out of the sea. In the process he deals with another pirate, whom he dispatches with a torch as we
hear his action theme beginning on D.

The saving of Quintus Arrius ("Rescue") marks the end of the battle
scene. Ben-Hur's theme, beginning on a B, is heard in the low strings (as
he dives under water for Arrius and takes him to a raft). The remainder
of the cue depicts the sinking of their ship (Roman Fleet theme), the
removal of the commander's armor (the Quintus Arrius theme in the
same key as when he donned the armor during "Battle Preparations"),
and the struggle to keep Arrius from committing suicide (rising chromatic line). At the close, Ben-Hur sinks exhausted, just as the Roman
ship sinks, accompanied by a variation of Roman Fleet in a low register.

The final cue in this section ("Roman Sails") begins when Ben-Hur
sees a ship. His anxiety concerning whether it is Roman (hence, a return
to slavery) is suggested by the reiteration of his cadential motive on the
pitch F and then, a tritone away, on B. Both phrases are played over an F
pedal. The recognition that the ship is from Rome brings another variation of Roman Fleet with a resigned character. The Rowing theme is
heard as they approach and later when Ben-Hur stares at the galley
slaves.

Rome

The music for Ben-Hur's stay in Rome is primarily diegetic. Roman
fanfares and a march, complete with dotted-rhythms and strong pulses,
accompany the victory parade. The celebration in which Quintus Arrius
announces his adoption of Ben-Hur has two excerpts of dance music.
The first, entitled "Fertility Dance," is a standard Bacchanal with energetic erotic dancing. Four flutes play a frantic melody that largely remains within a pentatonic scale. Three harps, a piano, and two marimbas
provide a quartal-chord accompaniment. The other dance music also
uses a small ensemble, including woodwind solos, two harps, and percussion. The light, sprightly dance tune and instrumentation suggests the
timbres of the observed harps and tibias.

The only scoring in Rome ("Nostalgia" and "Farewell to Rome") concludes this portion of the film. Initially, we see Judah wistfully fondling Esther's slave ring, while Esther's theme sounds (in G) for the first time since before the accident. As Arrius enters and senses that his newly adopted son is about to leave, Rózsa gives us one of the most sensitive musical moments of the film. A new theme appears in the cellos that centers on the upward leap of a major seventh and a quick ornamental turn (Example 5.11). The melody includes pitches (marked with an x) found in the altered version of Ben-Hur's theme (pitches 4-9, Example 4.4b). The cadence also resembles the cadential motion of his theme. The harmony contains a series of expressive major-seventh chords. At the conclusion, the Anno Domini motto chords sound softly in C, marking the end of his exile.

Example 5.11. "Farewell to Rome," Melody.

Judea

Ben-Hur's return to Judea initiates additional plot reversals. Like Messala, Ben-Hur is now a Roman citizen, has been successful in Rome, and has been stripped of many of his emotions. The barrenness of his spirit is mirrored visually by the desolate appearance of the once thriving House of Hur and musically by the extended moments with no scoring. The music for this portion of the film can be heard in two parts. Initially, there is a reprise of themes that have not been heard since the roof incident four years earlier. The second part occurs with the discovery that Miriam and Tirzah have leprosy. This brings about a harsh new melody and the first playing of Miriam's theme since the Overture.

Balthazar

Ben-Hur's arrival in Judea is set with three cues. The first two, "Judea" and "Balthazar," present a succession of five themes. The Judea theme maintains its introductory role (as at the beginnings of both the Christ and Ben-Hur expositions) and once again establishes the locale. Supported with F-minor triads, the melody is presented warmly with a variation of its countermotive (Example 5.2). In "Balthazar," the medley of themes resembles a mini-overture: Balthazar in F, Ben-Hur in D-flat, Esther in F, Balthazar in B-flat, and Christ in G. Except for Balthazar, all of these themes appear in key areas that match their appearances in the first portion of the film.

The third cue, "Balthazar's World," enters after an extended musical break. Set in Ilderim's tent, Balthazar recognizes Ben-Hur's hatred and urges him to adopt a forgiving attitude. The cue begins with the cadential motive of Hatred played relatively slowly by the English horn in C-sharp, Ben-Hur's key (Example 5.12). The repetition of the motive in the clarinet (m. 3) alters the theme so that the distinctive tritone becomes a perfect fifth. With the subdued presentation and modification of the Hatred motive, the music suggests that Balthazar is offering an alternative to hate. The cue continues with Balthazar's theme, Christ's theme (as he talks of the Messiah), and Balthazar's theme in D, its original key area.

Example 5.12. "Balthazar's World," Beginning.

Jerusalem

Ben-Hur takes leave of Ilderim's hospitality to return to Jerusalem and his home. "Homecoming" begins with an abbreviated statement of the altered Ben-Hur theme as he leaves the tent (Example 4.4b). The remainder of the cue is in an A-B-A' form. The A sections are statements of Judea in D. The first underscores Judah's arrival in Jerusalem, and the second begins when he reverently touches the mezuzah at the entrance to the House of Hur. The B section contains an extended setting of the House of Hur theme that includes quasi-canonic imitation between the oboe and the viola. The music fades once Judah enters the courtyard. The bleakness of the interior is in stark contrast to the earlier scenes in these locations. Music is withheld for an extended period and is conspicuously absent when Ben-Hur reunites with Esther and Simonides.

When Judah lifts Simonides, music reenters ("Memories") with a gentle string variation of the Ben-Hur theme (briefly in D-flat). The scene immediately cuts to the upstairs room where Ben-Hur and Esther first declared love. They meet again and repeat some of their earlier dialogue. Rózsa reinforces the parallel between these two moments by bringing back Esther's theme in the same key (C) and with a similar instrumentation (flute, harp, and the addition of string tremolos). When the scene begins, Ben-Hur is standing in the room deep in thought. Esther's theme enters with its second phrase, suggesting that he has been there for a while. The music deviates from the earlier cue when they kiss passionately, leading to a solo violin statement of the Esther theme.

The warm mood is broken when Esther mentions Messala. In a cue entitled "Hatred," the harmony shifts to Ben-Hur's D-flat, and variations of the Hatred and Esther themes are set in counterpoint (Example 5.13). Esther's melodic line centers on G, a tritone away from the prevailing harmonic center. When Esther mentions the savior, the first phrase of Christ's theme enters in C, but Judah quickly rejects the suggestion of hope. The cue ends darkly with dissonance and a motive from the desert march (Example 5.5a) after Esther refers to his sentence to the galley. In the room where they had declared love, hatred begins to drive them apart.

Example 5.13. Variations on Esther and Hatred.

Lepers

A stinger followed by the striking of a gong reflects the shock when a guard discovers that the prisoners Miriam and Tirzah are alive but stricken with leprosy ("Lepers"). The initial six-note chord combines two major triads separated by a tritone (G and D-flat), which contains all of the pitches of the chromatic theme other than C. The Leprosy theme (Example 5.14) exhibits several Roman features, including multiple tritones (marked with brackets) and second-beat accents. The melody, which encompasses the descent of a minor seventh, has two parts. The first is a quick four-note motive that recalls the countermotive in "Desperation" (Example 5.6b). In the third measure, the second statement of this motive elides with a new idea that resembles the descending tritone motive in Hatred, especially with its repetition in the last measure. The entire theme is restated a minor third higher when Drusus goes into the cell to see for himself.

Example 5.14. Leprosy Theme.

Released from prison, Miriam and Tirzah pass their former home on the way to the Valley of Lepers. Their chance encounter with Esther is supported musically by two successive cues, "Return" and "Promise" (Table 5.5). The Leprosy theme is heard at the beginning of "Return" when Miriam informs Esther about their condition. In this statement, the theme begins on an E, the theme's most characteristic pitch center. The harmony is more subdued than in "Lepers," but it still features a three-pitch imperfect quartal chord that creates a minor second and a tritone (see the top staff in Example 5.16).

Table 5.5. Outside the House of Hur

Cue	Theme	Key Center
Return	Leprosy	E
	Miriam	C/F
	Ben-Hur	C/C#
Promise	Esther	C#
	Miriam	D

Miriam's theme frames the remainder of the musical segment. The first of these is the most extended, a complete ABA' presentation beginning in C minor. The middle portion contains a canon between the oboe and cellos based on motives of the theme, and the return of A is in F, Miriam's original key in the Overture. When Miriam and Tirzah leave, the theme returns. After the first two phrases, the melody is treated freely, and the cue ends with the mood of quiet sadness.

The themes for Ben-Hur and Esther separate the two Miriam settings. Ben-Hur's theme sounds when he passes without seeing the women. The theme is initially in C, but then shifts to C-sharp with a wistful version in the clarinet; both statements use the altered version of the theme. Esther's theme, introduced by a solo cello, is also in C-sharp and enters just after Miriam recognizes that she loves Ben-Hur (beginning of "Promise"). The thematic material is varied as Esther struggles with making a promise not to tell Ben-Hur that she has seen his mother and sister. The painful decision is reflected in the dissonant harmony, which includes the bitonal combination of B-flat and A major triads.

Fulfilling her promise to Miriam, Esther later tells Ben-Hur that his mother and sister are dead. This prompts an intense cue ("Sorrow and

Intermission") with three thematic ideas. The opening contains an expressive string theme (Example 5.15). The first measure can be heard as a variation of the Friendship head motive, and the third measure foreshadows a motive that will accompany Christ on his death march (Example 5.20a). These two ideas will be combined into a single melody again after the Crucifixion (Example 4.7b). A passionate version of the Judea theme enters as Ben-Hur weeps while leaning against the mezuzah. In its final statement in the film (other than the entr'acte), the Judea theme returns to its original key of A. The Hatred theme follows immediately. Beginning in F, it moves through a *piu mosso* tempo and accelerates with repeated statements of the tritone cadential motion. A final harsh statement in the brass rises to a dramatic climax and cadences with the open fifth F - C.

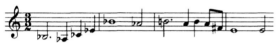

Example 5.15. Sorrow.

Bitter Triumph

Ben-Hur enters the Circus for the chariot race, a true test of Roman skill. With his victory, he is once again a Roman champion. But his triumph is empty, as he learns that his vengeance against Messala brings no resolution to his anger and that his mother and sister have leprosy. He reaches new depths of agony, just as Jesus is offering a new sense of hope to the world. Musically, Ben-Hur's triumph is reflected in the appearance of his theme in a Roman march. Subsequent cues reflect the bitterness that has consumed him. Particularly noteworthy is the diminished role of his theme for the remainder of the film. The action hero has given himself over to hatred.

Entr'acte

The Entr'acte is an abbreviated version of the Overture. The Anno Domini, Judea, and Esther themes are heard as before, but Miriam and Friendship are omitted. The other difference between the two is the coda. While the Overture begins in A and finishes quietly in E-flat, the coda of the Entr'acte, still using the Anno Domini theme, makes an emphatic cadence in A, thereby reaffirming the opening key of the film.

The pitch center A is also the primary key for the Hatred theme, which dominates this portion of the film.

Circus

The Circus brings about a number of fanfares (all moving in parallel triads) and two marches, both in A. The first march, "Panem et Circenses" (bread and circuses), is borrowed from *Quo Vadis*, where it was originally harmonized in F. The recasting of the march in A not only reinforces the pitch center of the Entr'acte and of Hatred, but also enables the second strain to be heard in Ben-Hur's key of C-sharp, thereby foreshadowing his victory. The second and more famous march, "Circus Parade" (commonly known as "Parade of the Charioteers"), has two thematic ideas that move in parallel triads. As noted in chapter 4, the melody of the A section (Example 4.8b), with its distinctive accent on the second beat, is a variation of Hatred (Example 4.6). The B section contains the Ben-Hur theme, reaffirming his Roman qualities. The climactic chariot race has no music.

The first scoring since intermission, over thirty minutes into this portion of the film, occurs when Ben-Hur comes to the dying Messala and learns that Miriam and Tirzah are lepers. Two cues frame the scene, "Bitter Triumph" and "Aftermath." Both present the Friendship theme in funeral settings, with slow tempos and chordal support in the trombones. Dissonances prevail, including an unsettling quartal chord (D, G, C) at the conclusion of "Bitter Triumph" and bitonal chords in "Aftermath." As Judah walks back into the arena, a muted trumpet plays the fanfare passage from "Circus Parade," mocking his hollow victory.

Valley of Lepers

Ben-Hur seeks his mother and sister in the Valley of Lepers. Here he sees Esther and confronts her about the deception, which he views as a betrayal. The three cues during this segment are "Valley of the Lepers," "The Search," and "The Uncleans" (Table 5.6). In all three, the appearances of the Leprosy theme recall the setting in "Lepers." The theme remains at the same pitch (outlining a G-diminished seventh chord), the orchestration is similar, and the harmonies incorporate the earlier three-pitch imperfect quartal chord.

Table 5.6. Valley of Lepers

Cue	Theme	Key Center
Valley of Lepers	Leprosy	E
	Chant theme	E/F
The Search	Chant theme	F/C
	Leprosy	E
	Desert motives	F
No Music		
The Uncleans	Leprosy	E
	Miriam	E

Other than a brief pause for a reel change, "Valley of the Lepers" and "The Search" can be heard as a single unit in an ABAC form. The A sections generate an ominous mood with statements of Leprosy supported by *sul ponticello* tremolos, muted brass, and colorful percussion, including the gong and vibraphone. The chordal harmony (Example 5.16) contains the pitches as in the cue "Lepers," but the lower register adds alternating fifths separated by a tritone: C-sharp and G. As a result, the opening harmony is an imperfect five-note quartal chord (E, A-sharp, D-sharp, G-sharp, C-sharp). The French horns intone a pedal on E with dotted rhythms, helping to define this as the central pitch.

Example 5.16. "Valley of Lepers," Harmony.

Several passages in these three cues suggest the proximity of Jesus to the Valley. The B section, which overlaps "Valley of the Lepers" and "The Search," features a chantlike recitation with a narrow range and parallel triadic harmonies, as will be heard with Christ's Sermon. In "Valley of the Lepers," the chords are second-inversion triads, and the melody lies within a major third. It is played twice, centering on E and then F, which clashes with the prevailing pedal E. The prominence of trombone, the frequent dissonance, and the plodding rhythmic pace suggest a dirge. Once Judah enters the valley (the beginning of the "The Search"), the somber melody expands its range, moves with parallel seventh chords, and assimilates a descending chromatic triplet that recalls the chromaticism of Ben-Hur's desert march (Example 5.17).

Example 5.17. "The Search," Opening.

There are several other musical references to Ben-Hur's earlier encounter with Christ; his later admission that he is still "thirsty" may be the link. After Esther enters (the C of ABAC form), Rózsa brings back the triplet figure from the episode at the well (Example 5.6a) and emphasizes the melodic fall of a minor third, which is also prominent in "Desert." These ideas are supported with a biting minor-second harmony.

When Miriam and Tirzah emerge from the cave, "The Uncleans" begins with a free treatment of the Leprosy theme that includes imitation with voices set a tritone apart (D-flat and G). Another reference to the nearness of Jesus can be heard in the accompaniment, as the violins quietly intone the first phrase of the Christ theme in tremolos. A full ABA statement of Miriam's theme follows in E, largely played by strings. The tone turns warmer when Esther assures Miriam that Ben-Hur is doing well. The imitative echoes return, and the theme even sprouts a brief violin solo.

Hope and Despair

The momentary intersection of the stories of Ben-Hur and Christ brings forth statements of the Christ, Balthazar, and Ben-Hur themes. Ben-Hur leaves the Valley angrily, which initiates the first of three successive cues, "Road of Sorrow," "The Mount," and "The Sermon." Initially, Judah's frustration is depicted with simultaneous minor and diminished triads on E (the chord contains both B and B-flat) under a distorted version of Miriam's theme. He comes to a stream near where people are gathering for Christ's sermon. Judah's recollection of a man who gave him water in the desert is musically supported by several statements of the Christ theme, first in F and then D. The first of these is preceded by one of the few variations given to Christ's thematic material, as the countermotive is altered to include an augmented-second interval and descending half steps.

The contrast between the joyful Balthazar and the bitter Judah is evident in their themes. A full sixteen-measure statement of Balthazar's theme in F is bathed in Christian warmth. Subsequently, Judah's emotional emptiness is suggested by a series of low-register chords, chromaticism, and the reiterated motto motive from Anno Domini in the violas. The distorted version of the Ben-Hur theme returns in F as he leaves.

Two thematic ideas accompany Christ's sermon. The introduction is provided by the final full appearance of the Anno Domini theme, now in F. Unlike its brash opening character, the passage is marked moderato e misterioso. Tremolo strings and subdued brass are the dominant timbres.

Just as we never see Christ's face in the film, we never hear his voice. For the sermon, Rózsa composed a chant-like passage supported by parallel second-inversion triads centered on E-flat, a traditional Christian key with three flats (representing the Trinity). The chant is clearly related to Christ's theme with its range and Phrygian mode, but the rhythms and declamation are dictated by the biblical text that Rózsa writes in the score beneath the chords (Example 5.18): "Blessed are the merciful, for they shall obtain mercy; blessed are the peacemakers, for they shall be called the children of God." This gentle reference to the Beatitudes is based on a misunderstanding. Clearly, Rózsa considered this moment to be Christ's Sermon on the Mount, but this was delivered on Mount Galilee several years earlier. The observed sermon takes place on Mount Olivet, where Christ taught during Passion Week.

Bless-ed   are   the   mer-   ci-   ful For they shall ob-tain   mer-cy

Example 5.18. "The Sermon."

After meeting with Pontius Pilate and disavowing his Roman heritage, Ben-Hur reaches an emotional low. He no longer blames Messala, but focuses his hatred on Rome. Symbolically, his home is still barren, and most of his dialogue with Esther has no musical support. Rózsa once again pinpoints a plot reversal with the cue "Frustration." In exasperation, Esther exclaims: "It's as though you had become Messala." As Ben-Hur reacts, Rózsa brings in the Hatred theme in its original key (A) and in a setting nearly identical to the moment when Messala first turned against Ben-Hur. The repeating descending tritone motive emphasizes Judah's current state. His choice—either hatred or love—is reflected in the music, as the English horn plays two phrases of Esther's theme in B-flat.

The music for "Frustration" continues into the next scene. Esther's return to the valley brings out the Leprosy theme with the key center (E) and the harmonization and foreboding accompaniment of "Valley of Lepers." Ben-Hur appears, and the cue entitled "Valley of the Dead" begins with the announcement that Tirzah is dying. His despair is underscored by a variation of the Leprosy theme (compare Example 5.19 with 5.14). After a momentary diversion to the Christ theme on F-sharp when Esther suggests taking them to see Christ, the Leprosy variant returns more harshly, supported by minor-second harmonic clashes.

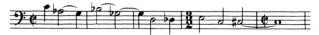

Example 5.19. Leper Theme Variation in "Valley of the Dead."

Tension is released when Judah comforts his mother, a moment that is accompanied by Miriam's theme in F-sharp. This theme is developed as Ben-Hur begins to look for his sister. The repetition of its third measure with parallel first-inversion triads and a countermelody is particularly striking. In "Tirzah Saved," the desperation of the search brings forth repetitions of Ben-Hur's head motive in its altered version alternating with a motive from Miriam. When he finds Tirzah, a statement of all three phrases of Ben-Hur's altered theme emerges. The momentary sense of triumph dissipates as the film cuts to their arrival at the empty streets of Jerusalem. A quiet bitonal chord and three statements of the Anno Domini motto chords with parallel tritones create an unnerving atmosphere.

Climax and Resolution

The stories of Ben-Hur and Christ merge when Jesus is sentenced to the cross. The Crucifixion and its aftermath provide the climactic moments of the film. With the healing of Miriam and Tirzah, Ben-Hur's fall from grace is reversed, and the resolution suggests hope for the world and happiness for Judah and Esther. Musically, the harshness of the Roman world dissipates, and love and redemption are reflected in the full orchestration, predominance of major triads, and the triumphal presentation of the Esther and Christ themes with voices.

Procession to Calvary

The six-minute sequence of Christ carrying his cross through the streets of Jerusalem has three impressive cues: "The Procession to Calvary," "The Bearing of the Cross," and "Recognition." In these, Rózsa creates an unrelenting sense of tragedy through pedal points on D, recurring D-minor chords, and the alternation of tension and resolution in two measure units (see Example 5.20a). Also contributing to the dirgelike character are the emphatic beats of low-pitch instruments and percussion on every half note.

"The Procession to Calvary" establishes the two main thematic ideas of the scene as a whole. The Procession theme contains a prominent descending tetrachord, a traditional symbol of pain and death (measure three of Example 5.20a). This simple idea is related to two other themes in the score. The Anno Domini motto heard at the onset of the film (descent and return of a major second) precedes the descending motion. Moreover, the four pitches of the tetrachord can generate the pitch content of the first two phrases of the Christ theme. While the Christ theme rises in hope, the procession descends in despair. Indeed, the third measure of the Procession theme can be heard as a variation of the second phrase in the Christ theme (note the pitches marked with an x in Example 5.20a). The Contrasting Procession theme also contains the motto gesture, linking it to both the Procession and Christ themes. (Example 5.20b is an expanded version of this theme from "The Bearing of the Cross.")

Example 5.20a. Procession Theme.

Example 5.20b. Contrasting Procession Theme.

In "The Procession to Calvary," passages with the Procession theme are heard four times. The first three are in successively higher registers. During the first contrasting section, the descending motive linked with the Hatred cadence (Example 5.4b) sounds in the bass register. The second contrasting section introduces rising sequences, and the third features chromatic variations of motives from both themes. The constant build-up of tension culminates in the anguished fourth statement of the Procession theme, now blaring in the low brass.

Example 5.21. Guard Whips Jesus.

"The Bearing of the Cross" underscores the film's shift from the spectacle of the procession to the more intimate depiction of Christ's suffering. Much of the same thematic material continues, but dissonances and chromaticism are intensified. After a two-measure statement of the Procession theme, the expanded version of the contrasting theme shown in Example 5.20b is played with parallel fourths. When a soldier whips Jesus, a bitonal chord sounds with roots separated by a tritone (Example 5.21). Added to this six-note chord is a half-step Scottish snap gesture in the bass that momentarily creates an eight-note chord with two minor seconds and three tritones.

When the procession resumes, the contrasting theme can be heard with a six-note descending chromatic ostinato in the rhythm of Example 5.4b. Eleven measures later, a chromatic variation of the Procession theme enters (Example 5.22) in which the accented E-flats and C-sharps clash with the underlying D pedal. The motion gradually descends chromatically encompassing the interval of a sixteenth, ending with the violin's lowest pitch, an open G. The cue concludes with another statement of both procession themes and a quick motive that falls a major seventh (a gesture associated with Roman cruelty).

Example 5.22. Altered Procession Theme.

The same material continues in "Recognition" with one major inter-
jection. Ben-Hur breaks through the crowd and offers water to the fallen
Jesus, a reversal of roles from their first meeting at the well. Rózsa highlights this connection by bringing back the Roman Guard theme from
the earlier scene (Example 5.6c). As before, it is presented canonically
with the two principal voices separated by a tritone. A brief statement of
the Christ theme follows, but when a soldier kicks the water and shoves
Judah aside, a bitonal chord (A-flat minor and G major triads) leads to a
final statement of the Guard theme. The Procession theme returns to
round off the scene, ending once again with the low open G.

Crucifixion

The Crucifixion segment contains two consecutive, but distinct cues.
The first is the most curious of the film. Entitled "Aftermath–New," it
was originally intended for the death of Messala. The score even retains
written references to moments in the earlier scene. Befitting its intended
placement, the cue centers on the Friendship and Hatred themes, music
that is associated with the relationship between Judah and Messala. The
extent of Rózsa's involvement in this choice for arguably the film's
most dramatic moment is uncertain. John B. Archibald decries the
choice as being made by "some minor functionary."[6] Regardless of the
intention for borrowing this cue, the presence of these themes at this
dramatic point elevates their stature, giving them symbolic weight as
representing human love and hate, flawed qualities that have led to this
moment.

If the decision was indeed made by a minor functionary, then he
must have had some knowledge of music. "Aftermath–New" is a well-
written cue and succeeds in this scene, both emotionally and musically.
The predominant timbres—a cello melody with trombone chords—are
appropriate for death. Moreover, the reiterated D in the bass sustains the
pitch center of the Procession, and the frequent clashes with E-flat recall
the dissonances observed in Example 5.20a. The cue opens with two
statements of the Hatred cadence motive, each beginning on an E-flat.
Following a brief sequential rise, the full Hatred theme is stated in D,
while the bass sustains an E-flat in a C-minor harmony.

The remainder of the cue is dominated by the "A" phrase of Friendship, which is presented in a variety of pitch centers. The initial statement of this theme is coordinated with Judah's appearance behind
Balthazar. Rózsa modifies the descending tritone of Hatred to a perfect
fifth, as he did during Balthazar's talk in Ilderim's tent (Example 5.12),

and uses it as a countermotive to Friendship. At Judah's recollection of Christ giving him water, a bitonal chord (A-flat minor and G major triads) and descending melodic material suggest his bitterness. The music turns even darker with Balthazar's recollection of the birth of Jesus. Low-register instruments predominate; the English horn plays the Friendship theme, bassoons repeat the Hatred motive, and trombones provide a chordal accompaniment along with a C pedal and strokes of the gong.

Just after Balthazar says "for this beginning," the cue entitled "Golgotha" begins. The thematic material, which is presented in a simple A-B-A form, shifts the focus from the reactions of Judah and Balthazar back to Jesus. The Christ theme and countermelody frame the cue, providing a sense of hope. The middle section underscores the movements of the Roman soldiers and reprises the Roman Guard theme harmonized with parallel imperfect quartal chords.

Resolution

The healing of Miriam and Tirzah and the vision of Christ's blood being carried in streams throughout the land resolve both the Ben-Hur and Christ stories. The cue "Miracle"[7] begins with the Christ countermotive in the low brass followed by the second and third phrases of the Christ theme. (The omission of the first phrase allows the melody to begin with the strong leap of a fourth.) A descending scale in the French horns adds to the joyfulness of the scene. After this material is repeated, the harmony shifts to B-flat for a full statement of the Christ theme. In its key and orchestration, the passage links back to the opening of the Overture. The cue closes with an energetic canon based on the countermotive.

In "Finale," the Ben-Hur and Friendship themes appear without their unpredictable or harsh qualities. Both have been musically resolved through Jesus, and the Christ theme follows each. The first of the Christ statements begins as we see Esther's image in a puddle of water. The symbolism of water has been prominent throughout the film; Judah received water from Christ and Quintus Arrius, Judah survived his slavery ordeal by leaping into water to rescue Arrius, Judah drinks water on his return to Judea, he complains about still being thirsty by the river near where Christ is about to give a sermon, he offers Christ water, and Christ's blood is carried in a stream. Esther's watery image is just one of her numerous links to Christ.

A reduced string ensemble performs the second statement of the Christ theme while Judah tells Esther of Christ's dying words. In quick succession, the Esther (D) and Miriam themes (C minor) enter, reflecting Judah's reunion with the spiritual women in his life. Reaffirming Esther's association with Christianity, the orchestra and a wordless choir repeat her theme. This leads directly to the Christ theme and countermotive with voices singing "Alleluia" and the vision of a shepherd leading his flock near the three crosses of Calvary.

The music comes to its final climax with the image of Michelangelo's *Creation*. The finale contrasts strongly with the Anno Domini at the beginning of the film. The harshness of brass has given way to the warmth of strings and voices, and the open-fifth harmonies and modal qualities have been replaced with triads and a full E-major final cadence. We have just entered the world of Christianity, Hollywood style.

Conclusion

Previous chapters have placed *Ben-Hur* and its music within the contexts of the traditions stemming from William Wallace's novel, the conventions of Hollywood's biblical epics, and Rózsa's development as a composer. Building on over twenty years of experience, Rózsa synthesized these divergent influences and crafted a masterful score that matches the monumental character of the film, provides an appropriate range of moods, and is remarkably unified, especially considering the length of the epic. Solomon places Rózsa's work in its cinematic historical position: "Rózsa ... created a classical perfection against which all other scores to films set in antiquity can be compared."[8]

The music for *Ben-Hur* is Rózsa's most celebrated artistic achievement. In many ways, Rózsa's music stands as the last major symphonic score of the opulent Golden Age; it received both critical and popular acclaim, a feat that was becoming increasingly rare during the 1950s. While numerous orchestral film scores appear in succeeding generations, notably after 1977, few have received similar dual recognition, and all have benefited from Rózsa's model. Over fifty years after its inception, the music for *Ben-Hur* still stands as one of Hollywood's greatest musical achievements.

NOTES

Chapter 1

1. Miklós Rózsa, *Double Life* (New York: Wynwood Press, 1982, rev. 1989).

2. Rózsa, *Double Life*, 98. The nursery tune referenced in the title is "Twinkle, Twinkle, Little Star."

3. Pentatonic scales contain five pitches that are most easily found by playing on the black keys of a piano. Traditional Western scales, called diatonic, have seven pitches.

4. Zoltán Kodály, "The Pentatonic Scale in Hungarian Folk Music" (1917-1929) in *The Selected Writings of Zoltán Kodály* (London: Boosey & Hawkes, 1964), 11.

5. A Scottish snap is a two-note dotted rhythm in which the first is short and accented, and the second is long and unaccented. This distinctive rhythmic idea is also called the Scotch snap or Lombard snap.

6. Rózsa, *Double Life*, 19.

7. Rózsa complained that Kodály only produced "miniature Kodálys out of all his pupils," *Double Life*, 34.

8. Nancy Jane McKenney, "The Chamber Music of Miklós Rózsa" (PhD diss., University of Kentucky, 2002), 62-69.

9. Rózsa, *Double Life*, 41.

10. Rózsa, *Double Life*, 40.

11. Quartal chords are built on intervals of fourths, rather than thirds as in triads. Typically, they are found with three or four pitches. By altering one of the intervals to a tritone, a composer creates an "imperfect" quartal chord. Quartal chords are often associated with pentatonic scales. The pitches of a five-note quartal chord produce a pentatonic scale. In practical usage, the two generally function independently.

12. Rózsa, *Double Life*, 28.

13. William H. Rosar, "Music for Martians: Schillinger's Two Tonics and Harmony of Fourths in Leith Stevens' Score for *War of the Worlds* (1953)," *The Journal of Film Music* 1, no. 4 (Winter 2006), 432.

14. Jan G. Swynnoe, *The Best Years of British Film Music: 1936-1958* (Suffolk: Boydell Press, 2002), 163.

15. Miklós Rózsa, "The Cinderella of the Cinema: An Evaluation of Film Music and a Review of Its Progress," *Music Educators Journal* 32, no. 3 (January-February 1946), 58.

16. Karol Kulik, *Alexander Korda: The Man Who Could Work Miracles* (New Rochelle, NY: Arlington House Publishers, 1975), 204.

17. The Seminar of Music, sponsored by the Hollywood Writers Mobilization, was held at the Beverly Hills Hotel on May 17, 1945. The unpublished proceedings are housed at the music library of the University of Southern California and were brought to my attention by Bill Rosar.

18. "Seminar of Music," 18.

19. Robert U. Nelson, "Film Music: Color or Line?," *Hollywood Quarterly* 2, no. 1 (October 1946), 57-65.

20. "Seminar of Music," 4-8.

21. Lawrence Morton, "Film Music of the Quarter," *Hollywood Quarterly* 5, no. 3 (Spring 1951), 285.

22. Rózsa, "The Cinderella of the Cinema," 58.

23. Rózsa, *Double Life*, 142.

24. Steven Dwight Wescott, "Miklós Rózsa: A Portrait of the Composer as Seen Through an Analysis of His Early Works for Feature Films and the Concert Stage" (PhD diss., University of Minnesota, 1990), 283-84.

25. Rózsa, *Double Life*, 168.

26. Wescott, "Miklós Rózsa," 413.

27. Elliott W. Galkin, *Notes*, Second Series 15, no. 4 (September 1958), 647.

28. Walter Simmons, *Voices in the Wilderness: Six American Neo-Romantic Composers* (Lanham, MD: Scarecrow Press, 2006).

29. Rózsa, *Double Life*, 233.

30. In a reversal of standard practice, passages from this concerto were later adapted into Rozsa's film score for *The Private Life of Sherlock Holmes* (1970).

31. Robin Holloway, *Essays and Diversions II* (Trowbridge, Wiltshire: Cromwell Press Ltd., 2007), 121.

32. Christopher Palmer, "Miklos Rozsa," *Pro Music Sana* 1, no. 1 (Spring 1972), 4.

33. Rózsa, *Double Life*, 213.

34. Michael Talbot, *Music & Letters* 53, no. 4 (October 1972), 468.

35. Terry Teachout, "Double Life of Miklós Rózsa," *Commentary* (December 2001), 62.

36. Wescott, "Miklós Rózsa," 461.

Chapter 2

1. Rózsa has divided his scoring into five phases based on the dominant genres: oriental, psychological, film noir, historic/biblical, and science fiction. I have combined the psychological and noir films because they were written during the same years and because the definition of film noir has been expanded to include psychological subjects. The science fiction phase begins in the 1960s, but the focus here is on films leading up to *Ben-Hur*, and the later works will be addressed only briefly.

2. Rózsa, *Double Life*, 210.

3. Swynnoe, *The Best Years of British Film Music*, 163.

4. Neo-tonality refers to the creation of tonal centers without relying on the dominant-seventh, which is essential to functional harmony.

5. Steven Dwight Wescott, "Miklós Rózsa: A Portrait," 264.

6. Morton, "Film Music of the Quarter," 285.

7. Rózsa, "The Film Composer: 1 Miklós Rózsa," an interview with Derek Elley, *Films and Filming* 23/8, no. 272 (May 1977), 23.

8. These divisions are adapted from categories defined by Jon Tuska, *Dark Cinema: American Film Noir in Cultural Perspective* (Westport, CT: Greenwood Press, 1984).

9. John B. Currie, "The Killers," *Film Music* VI, no. 1 (September-October 1946), 18.

10. Details on the craftsmanship of this score can be found in Frederick W. Sternfeld's "The Strange Music of Martha Ivers," *Hollywood Quarterly* 2, no. 3 (April 1947), 242-51.

11. Nelson, "Film Music: Color or Line?," 62.

12. For a fuller description of the theremin's impact on the film, see Hans W. Heinsheimer, *Menagerie in F Sharp* (Garden City, NY: Doubleday & Company, 1947), 223.

13. Rózsa, *Double Life*, 151.

14. Lawrence Morton, "Film Music Profile: Miklos Rozsa," *Film Music* X, no. 4 (March-April 1951), 5.

15. Rózsa, *Double Life*, 168.

16. The film was released in mono, so the first theatrical stereo film was *The Robe*, which came out six months later. DVD versions of *Julius Caesar* have restored the stereo sound.

17. Rózsa, *Double Life*, 158.

18. Christopher Palmer, *The Composer in Hollywood* (London: Marion Boyars, 1990), 208.

19. Morton, "Rozsa's Music for *Quo Vadis*," *Film Music* XI, no. 2 (November-December 1951), 11-13.

20. This melody, in both the original notation and a modern transcription, is the first example for the first volume of the *Norton Anthology of Western Music*, 6th ed., edited by J. Peter Burkholder and Claude V. Palisca (New York: W.W. Norton & Company, 2010).

21. Rózsa, *Double Life*, 190.

22.   Rózsa, "Julius Caesar," *Film Music* XIII, no. 1 (September-October 1953), 11.

23.   John Fitzpatrick, "First Notes on *Young Bess*," *Pro Musica Sana* 1, no. 1 (Spring 1972), 5.

24.   Jon Solomon, *The Ancient World in the Cinema* (New Haven, CT: Yale University Press, 2001), 139.

Chapter 3

1.   Solomon, *The Ancient World in the Cinema*, 202.

2.   Victor Davis Hanson, *Ripples of Battle* (New York: Doubleday, 2003), 137.

3.   David Mayer, *Playing Out the Empire: Ben-Hur and Other Toga Plays and Films, 1893-1908—A Critical Anthology* (London: Oxford University Press, 1994), 190.

4.   In the 1930s, the name was changed to Ben-Hur Life Association. The order was disbanded in 1988 when the organization was converted to a mutual insurance company. Today it is known as USA Life One Insurance Company of Indiana.

5.   Hammond Lamont, "The Winner in the Chariot Race," *The Nation*, no. 80 (February 1905), 183.

6.   Marcia L. Pentz-Harris, Linda Seger, and R. Barton Palmer, "Screening Male Sentimental Power in *Ben-Hur*," *Nineteenth-Century American Fiction on Screen*, edited by R. Barton Palmer (Cambridge: Cambridge University Press, 2007), 108.

7.   Hanson, *Ripples of Battle*, 141-42.

8.   Towers & Curran in New York published a piano score in 1902.

9.   Katherine Preston, "The Music of Toga Drama," *Playing Out the Empire: Ben-Hur and Other Toga Plays and Films, 1893-1908—A Critical Anthology*, edited by David Mayer (London: Oxford University Press, 1994), 24.

10.   Robert and Katharine Morsberger, *Lew Wallace: Militant Romantic* (New York: McGraw-Hill, 1980), 458.

11.   Preston, "The Music of Toga Drama," 25.

12.   Notably, a similar Arabian quality is absent from Rózsa's score for *Ben-Hur* despite the prominence of Balthasar and Sheik Ilderim.

13.   Rózsa, "The Cinderella of the Cinema," 15.

14.   A Devadasi is associated with Hindu practices. In contemporary thought, a Devadasi is often equated with prostitution, but for Wallace, who described an "army" of them in the novel, the term simply meant a temple-dancer.

15.   Morsberger, *Lew Wallace: Militant Romantic*, 464.

16.   Morsberger, *Lew Wallace: Militant Romantic*, 465.

17.   Hanson, *Ripples of Battle*, 141.

18.   *New York Times*, December 3, 1899, 18.

19.   Quoted in Morsberger, *Lew Wallace: Militant Romantic*, 458.

20.   Martin Miller Marks, *Music and the Silent Film: Contexts and Case Studies, 1895-1924* (New York: Oxford University Press, 1997), 76-92.

21.   The film, given the title "Ben-Hur 1907," can be seen in its entirety on YouTube.

22.   King Vidor, *A Tree Is a Tree* (New York: Harcourt Brace, 1953), 20-21.

23.   The 1959 version also avoids showing the front of Christ and pays tribute to the earlier film with the close-up of Christ's hand on the cross at the climactic moment of the film.

24.   Vidal made his remarks on the documentary video *The Celluloid Closet* (1995).

25.   For details of criticisms of the film, see Morsberger, *Lew Wallace: Militant Romantic*, 484.

26.   *Variety*, November 18, 1959, 1.

27.   François Truffaut, *Hitchcock* (New York: Simon & Schuster, 1966), 13.

28.   George Lucas used the soundtrack of *Ben-Hur* while watching the images during production.

29.   Rózsa, *Double Life*, 191.

Chapter 4

1.   Solomon, *The Ancient World in the Cinema*, 5.

2.   Solomon, *The Ancient World in the Cinema*, 323-24.

3.   The image is shown as Plate 2B in Curt Sachs, *The Rise of Music in the Ancient World East and West* (New York: W.W. Norton & Company, 1943).

4.   "*Quo Vadis* at the Regent," *Moving Picture World* (February 7, 1914), 680.

5.   Ibid.

6.   A Cornicen was a junior office in the Roman army that played the Cornu, a brass instrument shaped like the letter G. The bucina has a similar shape, but is thinner.

7.   Solomon, *The Ancient World in the Cinema*, 157.

8.   Solomon, *The Ancient World in the Cinema*, 42.

9.   Sanya Shoilevska Henderson notes that one of the reasons that "attracted North to score *Spartacus* was the possibility to experiment with all kinds of exotic ethnic instruments and various unusual combinations of instrumental groups within a large symphonic orchestra." *Alex North, Film Composer* (Jefferson, NC: McFarland & Company, 2003), 131.

10.   Rózsa, "The Music in *Quo Vadis*," *Film Music* XI, no. 2 (November-December 1951), 4.

11.   Jon Solomon, "The Sounds of Cinematic Antiquity," *Classics and Cinema*, edited by Martin M. Winkler (Lewisburg, PA: Bucknell University Press, 1991), 269-70.

12.   Steven Wescott argues that this should not be interpreted as Phrygian, but as an example of Hungarian modality in "Miklós Rózsa's *Ben Hur*: The Musical-Dramatic Function of the Hollywood Leitmotiv," *Film Music* I, edited by Clifford McCarty (New York: Garland Publishing, 1989), 206. Without disagreeing with his astute observation, I believe that, within the context of the film set in antiquity, the melody will be heard as Phrygian, and that this was the composer's intention.

13.   Wescott's "Miklós Rózsa's *Ben Hur*" refers to this extension as "additionalism," and describes the technique's role in the score, 202-204.

14.   The cell motive has three pitches: a perfect fourth or fifth and an intervening major second. See Example 2.1.

Chapter 5

1.   Ralph Erkelenz, "*Ben-Hur*: A Tale of the Score," *Pro Musica Sana* 5/1, no. 61 (Spring 2005), 1-29; "Part Two" 5/2, no. 62 (Spring 2006), 3-36; "Part Three" 6/1, no. 63 (Spring 2007), 4-39; "Part Four" 7/1, no. 65 (Spring 2009), 3-32; and "Part Five" 7/2, no. 66 (Fall 2009), 3-49.

2.   In an imperfect quartal chord, one or more of the perfect fourths is expanded to an augmented fourth (tritone).

3.   Bitonality is a harmonic device associated with modern music in which two distinct tonal centers are present at the same time. In this instance, the term designates two ongoing pitch centers, but bitonal can also refer to a chord containing two unrelated triads.

4.   Also known as a false relation, the term cross-relation designates a nonmelodic chromatic shift in adjacent chords. The juxtaposition of D and F major triads, for example, will have an F-sharp in the initial chord and an F-natural in the second. Since this breaks the rules of traditional part writing, the sound will suggest an earlier time period.

5.   Wescott ties this figure to an earlier chromatic descent in the desert march and identifies it as belonging to a significant group of motives. "Miklós Rózsa's *Ben-Hur*," 196.

6.   John B. Archibald, "Reunions with Old Friends (Recurring Thematic Materials in Herrmann, Rozsa and Newman)," *Pro Musica Sana*, nos. 39-40 (Fall 1983), 4.

7.   The final film version of this cue is not contained in any of the extant scores. An excellent summary of the numerous versions of the film's final musical moments can be found in Erkelenz, *Pro Musica Sana* 7/2, no. 66 (Fall 2009), 41-47.

8.   Solomon, "The Sounds of Cinematic Antiquity," 275.

BIBLIOGRAPHY

Archibald, John B. "Reunions with Old Friends (Recurring Thematic Materials in Herrmann, Rozsa and Newman)," *Pro Musica Sana*, nos. 39-40 (Fall 1983): 3-9.

Auvil, Adrianne M. "A Survey of the Evolution and Use of Quartal and Quintal Sonorities, 1890-1960." PhD diss., Eastman School of Music of the University of Rochester, 1973.

Bick, Sally. "'Of Mice and Men': Copland, Hollywood, and American Musical Modernism." *American Music* 23, no. 4 (Winter 2005): 426-72.

Brown, Royal S. *Overtones and Undertones: Reading Film Music*. Berkeley: University of California Press, 1994.

Burt, George. *The Art of Film Music*. Boston: Northeastern University Press, 1994.

Cooper, David. *Bernard Herrmann's* The Ghost and Mrs. Muir: *A Film Score Guide*. Lanham, MD: Scarecrow Press, 2005.

Currie, John B. "The Killers," *Film Music* VI, no. 1 (September-October 1946): 18.

Darby, Ken. *Hollywood Holyland: The Filming and Scoring of The Greatest Story Ever Told*. Lanham, MD: Scarecrow Press, 1992.

Darby, William, and Jack Du Bois. *American Film Music: Major Composers, Techniques, Trends, 1915-90*. Jefferson, NC: McFarland & Company, 1990.

Daubney, Kate. *Max Steiner's* Now, Voyager: *A Film Score Guide*. Westport, CT: Greenwood Press: 2000.

Doeckel, Ken "Miklos Rozsa." *Films in Review* 16, no. 9 (November 1965): 536-48.

———. "The Four Concertos of Miklos Rozsa." *Pro Musica Sana* 1, no. 4 (Winter 1972-3): 4-11.

Elley, Derek. "The Film Composer: 1 Miklós Rózsa," *Films and Filming* 23, no. 8 (May 1977): 20-24.

―――. "The Film Composer: 1 Miklós Rózsa," *Films and Filming* 23, no. 9 (June 1977): 30-34.

Erkelenz, Ralph. "*Ben-Hur*: A Tale of the Score," *Pro Musica Sana* 5/1, no. 61 (Spring 2005), 1-29; "Part Two" 5/2, no. 62 (Spring 2006), 3-36; "Part Three" 6/1, no. 63 (Spring 2007), 4-39; "Part Four" 7/1, no. 65 (Spring 2009), 3-32; and "Part Five" 7/2, no. 66 (Fall 2009), 3-49.

Feisst, Sabine M. "Arnold Schoenberg and the Cinematic Art." *The Musical Quarterly* 83, no. 1 (Spring 1999): 93-113.

Fitzpatrick, John. "First Notes on *Young Bess*." *Pro Musica Sana* 1, no. 1 (Spring 1972): 5-8.

Fox, Barbara Beeghly. "Obsession and Crisis: Film Music and Narrative in *Double Indemnity* (1944), *Laura* (1944), and *Psycho* (1960)." Master's thesis, University of Nevada, Reno, 2005.

Frigyesi, Judit. "Béla Bartók and the Concept of Nation and Volk in Modern Hungary," *Musical Quarterly* 78, no. 2 (1994): 255-87.

―――. "The Aesthetic of the Hungarian Revival Movement." *Retuning Culture: Musical Changes in Central and Eastern Europe*, edited by Mark Slobin. Durham, NC: Duke University Press, 1996, 54-75.

―――.*Béla Bartok and Turn-of-the Century Budapest*. Berkeley: University of California Press, 1998.

Galkin, Elliott W. "Miklós Rózsa: String Quartet, op. 22, 1950." *Notes*, Second Series 15, no. 4 (September 1958): 647.

Gorbman, Claudia. *Unheard Melodies: Narrative Film Music*. Bloomington: Indiana University Press, 1987.

Gough-Yates, Kevin. "The European Film Maker in Exile in Britain 1933-1945." PhD diss., Open University (United Kingdom), 1991.

Hanson, Victor Davis. *Ripples of Battle*. New York: Doubleday, 2003.

Heckel, Frank. "Miklos Rozsa," *Filmmusik* 8, no. 12 (1982): 12-22.

Heinsheimer, Hans W. *Menagerie in F Sharp*. Garden City, NY: Doubleday & Company, 1947.

Henderson, Sanya Shoilevska. *Alex North, Film Composer*. Jefferson, NC: McFarland & Company, 2003.

Hickman, Roger. *Reel Music: Exploring 100 Years of Film Music*. New York, W.W. Norton, 2006.

―――. "Wavering Sonorities and the Nascent Film Noir Musical Style," *The Journal of Film Music* 2, nos. 2-4 (Winter 2009): 165-74.

Holloway, Robin, *Essays and Diversions II*. Trowbridge, Wiltshire: Cromwell Press Ltd., 2007.

Horton, Robert. "Music Man: Miklos Rozsa," *Film Comment* 31, no. 6 (November 1995): 2-4.

Huntley, John. *British Film Music*. London: Arno Press & The New York Times, 1972.

Kalinak, Kathryn. *Settling the Score: Music and the Classical Hollywood Film*. Madison: University of Wisconsin Press, 1992.

Karlin, Fred. *Listening to Movies: The Film Lover's Guide to Film Music*. New York: Schirmer Books, 1994.

Kodály, Zoltán. "The Pentatonic Scale in Hungarian Folk Music." *The Selected Writings of Zoltán Kodály*. London: Boosey & Hawkes, 1964, 11-23.

Koldys, Mark. "Miklos Rozsa and *Ben-Hur*," *Pro Musica Sana* 3, no. 3 (Fall 1974): 3-30.

Kulik, Karol. *Alexander Korda: The Man Who Could Work Miracles*. New Rochelle, NY: Arlington House Publishers, 1975.

Lack, Russell. *Twenty Four Frames Under*. London: Quartet Books, 1997.

Lamont, Hammond. "The Winner in the Chariot Race," *The Nation*, no. 80 (February 1905): 183.

Manvell, Roger, and John Huntley. *The Technique of Film Music*. London: Focal Press, 1957.

Marks, Martin Miller. *Music and the Silent Film: Contexts and Case Studies, 1895-1924*. New York: Oxford University Press, 1997.

Mayer, David. *Playing Out the Empire: Ben-Hur and Other Toga Plays and Films, 1893-1908—A Critical Anthology*. London: Oxford University Press, 1994.

McKenney, Nancy Jane. "The Chamber Music of Miklós Rózsa." PhD diss., University of Kentucky, 2002.

Morsberger, Robert E., and Katharine M. Morsberger. *Lew Wallace: Militant Romantic*. New York: McGraw-Hill, 1980.

Morton, Lawrence. "An Interview with George Antheil." *Film Music Notes* 10 (November-December 1950): 4-7.

———. "Film Music of the Quarter," *Hollywood Quarterly* 5, no. 3 (Spring 1951): 282-88.

———. "Film Music Profile: Miklós Rózsa," *Film Music* X, no. 4 (March-April 1951): 4-6.

———. "Rozsa's Music for *Quo Vadis*," *Film Music* XI, no. 2 (November-December 1951): 11-13.

Nelson, Robert. "Film Music: Color or Line?" *Hollywood Quarterly* 2, no. 1 (October 1946): 57-65.

Palmer, Christopher. "Miklos Rozsa," *Pro Music Sana* 1, no. 1 (Spring 1972): 2-5.

———. *The Composer in Hollywood*. London: Marion Boyars, 1990.

———. *Miklós Rózsa: A Sketch of His Life and Work*. London: Breitkopf & Härtel, 1975.

Pentz-Harris, Marcia L., Linda Seger, and R. Barton Palmer. "Screening Male Sentimental Power in *Ben-Hur*." *Nineteenth-Century American Fiction on Screen*, edited by R. Barton Palmer. Cambridge: Cambridge University Press, 2007, 106-32.

Prendergast, Roy. *Film Music: A Neglected Art*, 2nd ed. New York: W.W. Norton, 1992.

Preston, Katherine. "The Music of Toga Drama." *Playing Out the Empire: Ben-Hur and Other Toga Plays and Films, 1893-1908—A Critical Anthology*, edited by David Mayer. London: Oxford University Press, 1994, 23-29.

Raksin, David. "Film Music Today and Tomorrow." Undated, unpublished manuscript, Ingolf Dahl Collection, University of Southern California.

Rosar, William H. "Music for Martians: Schillinger's Two Tonics and Harmony of Fourths in Leith Stevens' Score for *War of the Worlds* (1953)," *The Journal of Film Music* 1, no. 4 (Winter 2006): 395-436.

Rózsa, Miklós. "The Cinderella of the Cinema: An Evaluation of Film Music and a Review of Its Progress," *Music Educators Journal* 32, no. 3 (January-February 1946): 15-17, 58.

———. "The Music in *Quo Vadis*," *Film Music* XI, no. 2 (November-December 1951): 4-10.

———. "More Music for Historical Films," *Film Music* XII, no. 2 (November-December 1952): 13-17.

———. "*Julius Caesar*," *Film Music* XIII, no. 1 (September-October 1953): 7-13.

———. "*Lust for Life*," *Film Music* XVI, no. 1 (Fall 1956): 3-6.

———. *Double Life*. New York: Wynwood Press, 1982; rev. 1989.

Schneider, David E. *Bartók, Hungary, and the Renewal of Tradition: Case Studies in the Intersection of Modernity and Nationality*. Berkeley: University of California Press, 2006.

"Seminar of Music," sponsored by the Hollywood Writers Mobilization, May 17, 1945. The unpublished proceedings are held at the music library of the University of Southern California.

Simmons, Walter. *Voices in the Wilderness; Six American Neo-Romantic Composers*. Lanham, MD: Scarecrow Press, 2006.

Solomon, Jon. "The Sounds of Cinematic Antiquity," 264-81 in *Classics and Cinema*, edited by Martin M. Winkler. Lewisburg, PA: Bucknell University Press, 1991.

———. *The Ancient World in the Cinema*. New Haven, CT: Yale University Press, 2001.

Steiner, Fred. *The Making of an American Film Composer: A Study of Alfred Newman's Music in the First Decade of the Sound Era*. PhD diss., University of Southern California, 1981.

Sternfeld, Frederick W. "The Strange Music of Martha Ivers," *Hollywood Quarterly* 2, no. 3 (April, 1947): 242-51.

Sullivan, Jack. *Hitchcock's Music*. New Haven, CT: Yale University Press, 2006.

Swynnoe, Jan G. *The Best Years of British Film Music: 1936-1958*. Suffolk: Boydell Press, 2002.

Teachout, Terry. "Double Life of Miklós Rózsa," *Commentary* (December 2001): 62-64.

Truffaut, François. *Hitchcock*. New York: Simon & Schuster, 1966.

Tuska, Jon. *Dark Cinema; American Film Noir in Cultural Perspective*. Westport, CT: Greenwood Press, 1984.

Vidor, King. *A Tree Is a Tree*. New York: Harcourt Brace, 1953.

Wagner, Hansjörg. "Miklos Rozsa," *Filmmusik* 11 (July 1984): 8-21.

Wescott, Steven Dwight. "Miklós Rózsa's *Ben Hur*: The Musical-Dramatic Function of the Hollywood Leitmotiv," *Film Music I*, edited by Clifford McCarty. New York: Garland Publishing, 1989: 183-207.

————. *Miklós Rózsa: A Portrait of the Composer as Seen Through an Analysis of His Early Works for Feature Films and the Concert Stage*. PhD diss., University of Minnesota, 1990.

————. "Rózsa, Miklós" in *The New Grove Dictionary of Music*, edited by Stanley Sadie. London: Macmillan Publishers, 2001.

Wiegandt, Matthias. "Vom Jungle Book zum Asphalt Jungle: Miklós Rózsas Filmmusik der vierzieger Jahre," 119-158 in *Emigrierte Komponisten in der Medienlandschaft des Exils 1933-1945*, edited by Nils Grosch, Joachim Lucchesi, and Jürgen Schebera. Kurt-Weill-Gesellschaft Dessau, Band 2. Stuttgart: M & P Verlag, 1998.

Winters, Ben. *Erich Wofgang Korngold's* The Adventures of Robin Hood: *A Film Score Guide*. Lanham, MD: Scarecrow Press, 2007.

INDEX

ABOUT THE AUTHOR

Roger Hickman received a PhD in musicology from UC Berkeley and is currently a full professor at The Bob Cole Conservatory of Music at California State University, Long Beach. He is the author of the textbook *Reel Music: Exploring 100 Years of Film Music* and has contributed to several other music history and humanities texts. Articles on a variety of subjects have appeared in *The Music Review*, *The Musical Quarterly*, *The Journal of Film Music*, *Early Music*, and *The New Grove Dictionary of Music*. The author also remains active as a conductor and is currently the music director for the Long Beach Ballet.

CPSIA information can be obtained at www.ICGtesting.com
Printed in the USA
BVOW040828190312

285319BV00005B/1/P